In the Shadow of the
Golden Thirteen

"A Nice Negro Story!"

Gerald A. Collins

1st WORLD
PUBLISHING

In the Shadow of the Golden Thirteen

Gerald A. Collins

Copyright © 2023 by Gerald A. Collins

Published by 1st World Publishing
P.O. Box 2211, Fairfield, Iowa 52556
tel: 641-209-5000 • fax: 866-440-5234
web: www.1stworldpublishing.com

First Edition
ISBN Softcover: 978-1-4218-3542-6
ISBN Hardcover: 978-1-4218-3543-3
LCCN: Library of Congress Cataloging-in-Publication Data

Front Cover Photo: Golden Thirteen Members with escort officers Lieutenants Maxwell Allen and Gerald Collins (author) and Lieutenant (j.g.) Bruce Martin – ships company (*All Hands Magazine (NH 1234 courtesy of the Naval History & Heritage Com.)*

Table of Contents

Dedication

To all those who served with me on the staff of Navy Recruiting Area Five, Great Lakes, during the period 1980-1982 and assisted in bringing about the at-sea reunion cruise onboard the USS Kidd (DDG-993) to honor the Golden Thirteen, the first African Americans regularly commissioned as officers in the United States Navy.

It is also dedicated to other minorities and women officers Karen Roach, Lynn Vaughn Allen, and Sandra Regan, who endured the undeserved wrath and career destruction that literally began in the shadow of the Golden Thirteen cruise; less than six months after the event which had the purpose of showing the positive progress of the Navy in the areas of race relations and equal opportunity.

Thanks, also, to Dan Goldberg, author of *The Golden Thirteen: How Black Men Won the Right to Wear Navy Gold*, Beacon press, May 2020, and LCDR Reubein Keith Green, USN (Ret.), author of *Black Officer, White Navy*, CreateSpace Independent Publishing Platform, North Charleston, South Carolina, 2017. It was their publications that reignited my desire to finally tell my story.

Finally, it is dedicated to my wife, Margaret, and our children, Michele and Asim, who watched as their husband and father struggled in the aftermath of events that destroyed his career and turned our world upside down.

Gerald A. Collins
Author

Prelude

In 1970, Elmo Zumwalt became the Chief of Naval Operations (CNO). At the age of forty-nine, he was the youngest CNO to that time in United States Navy history. A search of the many quotes attributed to the admiral revealed a remark, from Edmund Burke, which said, *"All that is necessary for the triumph of evil is that good men do nothing"* https://www.brainyquote.com/quotes/edmund_burke_377528.

I have heard many African Americans who served in the aftermath of Zumwalt's tenure say, *"That statement could be said to be the theme of his tenure."* Based upon my own Navy experience, I would agree.

From September 1965 through December 1989, I served directly in or was associated with the United States Navy. First as an enlisted, and later, in 1977, as an officer. *In the Shadow of the Golden Thirteen, A Nice Negro Story* is the story of my experiences attempting to achieve recognition for the men identified as the first African American commissioned and warrant officers in the United States Navy. It is also the story of how my seemingly innocent idea for recognition of their and other minority accomplishments heralded the destruction of my own career by some who considered their accomplishments as little more than "*a nice Negro story.*"

In retrospect, I must state, I am extremely proud of my association with the Golden Thirteen story. That pride stems from letters and remarks like this excerpted from one member, Mr. John Reagan, dated April 27, 1982, in which he stated: "*I am still 10 kilometers high from that terrific 'Golden Thirteen' reunion at sea. It is near impossible to express how much I appreciated the terrific job you did with and for us and indeed for the Navy and recruiting service.*"

Despite the personal hurt I have endured these past decades as a result of the reunion, I can think of few things in my life that mean more. - GAC

Chapter 1

Reenlistment, Commissioning, SWOS

I originally enlisted in the United States Navy in 1965, just as the war in Vietnam was beginning to take its heaviest human toll. I joined the Navy largely due to the influence of my mother, Grace Collins, and my brother, Glover F. Collins, Jr; both now deceased.

My mother worked for nearly thirty-five years as a clerk in various Navy departments at old Main Navy on Constitution Avenue in Washington, DC. My brother served in the Navy as an enlisted man for nearly 25 years, retiring as a Senior Chief, Boiler Technician.

Upon enlisting, I qualified for an A School. I had hoped to become a Photographer's Mate. I went through Basic Training at Great Lakes Naval Training Station, just outside of North Chicago, Illinois. I enlisted as Aviation Photographer's Mate Technician Apprentice. While in Basic Training, my dream of becoming a Photographer's Mate died when I learned that I suffered with a lazy eye. I was offered and accepted another A School billet, this time as a Communications Technician (CT) "A"-Branch Apprentice. Upon graduation, I learned that there was no billet open for my rate. So, I was sent to the *USS DOUGLAS H. FOXX (DD-779)*, for pre-school indoctrination (PSI). Once I arrived on the *FOXX*, I realized that PSI was a means of stashing bodies until school seats became available. With Vietnam ramping up, it made sense. Despite being assigned to the deck force my entire time on board, I enjoyed being on the FOXX. It gave me my first glimpse of overseas duty when we sailed into Ocho Rios, Jamaica; Porto-Au-Prince, Haiti; and Guantánamo, Cuba. I was fascinated because I had never experienced such diverse societies and peoples. When I arrived at Communications Technician (CT) "A" School in Bainbridge, MD, I was ready for my "next great Navy adventure."

I began classes in June and graduated in August 1966. Little did I know that my "adventure" was to be assigned to the Staff, Commander-In-Chief US Naval Forces Europe, Navy Security Group Unit Detachment, Europe, aka CINCUS-NAVEUR, NAVSECGRUDET, London, England. My assignment lasted exactly two years. I was so influenced by that experience I wrote a book about it. The book titled *Douglas House!* was published in 2003 by Groundbreaking Press. It was truly my coming-of-age story. At the end of my tour in London, despite being newly married, expecting a child, and enamored with England, I decided to return to the States.

When I returned, I was a Second Class CT with orders to Headquarters, Naval Security Group Detachment Washington, DC.

Despite having a Top-Secret special intelligence clearance, I was assigned to work outside my rate as the Petty Officer in Charge of the Gatehouse. Others, whites, with whom I had worked in London, continued to work in our rate in the classified communications center. That one thing, combined with other forms of bigotry and discrimination I had witnessed, confirmed my decision to leave the Navy. I left the Navy in September 1969, convinced there had to be a better path in life for me. Ironically, one of those paths I found attractive was possibly becoming a naval officer. When I left the Navy, I turned my attention to getting my degree. And I went to work in broadcast communications. Two years later, I had my bachelor's degree and was well on my way to acquiring my master's.

In 1972, just after I was awarded my undergraduate degree, I began hearing about Navy direct appointment programs, and reading about Vice Admiral Zumwalt, his "Z-grams," and the tangible differences he was making in the lives of the average sailors. His activities convinced me to reenlist in the naval reserves in late 1974 with the aim of becoming an officer. I was sworn in as a Petty Officer Second Class. Once sworn in, I applied for a direct appointment public affairs reserve commission. In the interim, while awaiting that decision, I was ordered to attend the Enlisted Navy Recruiting Orientation (ENRO) Course in Pensacola, Florida. However, before I could execute orders as a Petty Officer, I was sworn in as an ensign. Despite being an ensign, I was ordered to execute the ENRO orders. My arrival at ENRO as an ensign instead of a Second-Class Petty Officer created a minor stir.

I could not stay in the enlisted barracks. So, they adjusted my orders, increased my per diem, and put me up in a hotel until a place in the Bachelor Officers' Quarters could be found. I thoroughly enjoyed my first taste of being treated as an officer!

Chapter 2

Surface Warfare School (Basic) – No Source Program

When I returned from ENRO, I was detailed to NRD Washington. It was at the NRD that I was encouraged to request recall to active duty. After some thought, it occurred to me that while recall would be great, the thing to do to really secure my future as an active-duty officer was to request recall *and* a change of designator from public affairs (1655) to unrestricted line (1100). So that is what I did. To the surprise of all, my request was approved.

In the fall of 1977, I was ordered to Newport, Rhode Island to attend Surface Warfare Officers (Basic) School (SWOS) and Communications Officer (Basic). Amid the excitement over my personal accomplishments, reality stepped in.

Just before going to SWOS, I lost my younger sister, Joanne. My parents had eleven children. Over the years, two of the eleven had died in early childhood. Nine of the eleven grew to adulthood. I was the seventh, and Joanne was the eighth child born to my parents, Glover, and Grace Collins.

Joanne's death was particularly hard because she was just twenty-eight when she passed as a result of sarcoidosis. My parents were devastated. Just after Joanne's death, my mother learned she had breast cancer. I did not learn of my mother's personal ordeal until after I finished SWOS.

To say that SWOS was a reality check would be an understatement. I was thirty-two when I reported. How I came to be at SWOS is a story in itself.

Returning home in 1968, after my initial enlistment, I was certain that I did not want to work any longer as a Communications Technician or anything related. During my last year of enlisted active duty, I discovered that Radio/TV Journalism was what I felt called to do. So, I focused my efforts on enhancing my knowledge and skills in that area and getting an undergraduate degree.

While using the GI Bill to finish college, I was fortunate enough to get an internship at a local TV station. The program lasted two years. I was working in television and radio production, operating studio and still cameras, processing 35mm film and floor directing. It was an exciting time.

While working at a local Washington. DC, television station, I learned from a friend, Sherman Jones, that the Navy had a direct appointment Public Affairs Officer (PAO) program. I applied and to my surprise, I was accepted as a reserve PAO.

Once I was sworn in, I was assigned to work with Navy Recruiting District, Washington DC. It was there that I learned that I could be recalled to active duty. Of course, I applied, but was initially turned down. It was after that

I learned that one could change their designator code (occupational specialty code). So, I put two and two together and requested a change of designator. As the saying goes, be careful what you ask for. I got the change of designator from reserve PAO to unrestricted line. And, the bonus, so to speak, was orders to SWOS.

When I got to SWOS, I was pleased to be in the middle of a group of guys who had just graduated from the academy and various ROTC/OCS programs. In many ways, I felt I had managed to lop ten years off my age. In other ways, I responded and acted like the "older" man that I was.

When I arrived at SWOS, I had not taken a math or science related course since high school, fifteen years before. As can be imagined, I failed all courses that remotely involved math or science.

I went before more academic review boards than I care to admit. During one of the boards, one of my instructors noted the rate of my failings, and my age difference. During that review, he asked a question I had never heard before. He asked, "Mr. Collins, what is your source program?" I had not a clue what he was asking. Then he rephrased it. "How did you get to be an officer?"

When I told him the story of my commissioning, he simply said, "No wonder you are having issues." He went on, "You are only seeing these materials for the first time. And it is showing in your grades." He continued, "Most of your peers have seen this stuff at least once before in college or at the academy. Your grades are just barely failing. The Navy should not have put you through this. And we are going to fix it."

I had no idea what he was suggesting. I was allowed to finish SWOS, after which I went on to Communications Officer School, and sent to a reserve destroyer out of Newport, RI, the USS VOGELGESANG (DD-682).

Onboard, I served for six months as the First Division Officer, stood in port and underway watches, and got a taste of engineering watches. At the end of that stint, I returned to SWOS. Later, when I was asked, "What is your source program, I would proclaim, "SWOS." I know that answer baffled many people. I rarely told the story behind my response.

During my initial time at SWOS, I was ashamed of my failing. Once I returned to SWOS from VOGELSANG, I reached out to my oldest brother, Francis, a Senior Chief Boiler Technician stationed at Concord Naval Weapons Station. Initially, he was harsh in his comments to me regarding my "failing." But then he became extremely helpful. Long distance, he helped me to understand the steam plant, navigation, etc.

The best advice he gave me came at the end of an hour's long long-distance when he said, "You should not be having difficulty with that or any of your classes." Then he said, "What is your learning style?" I was baffled and responded, "What do you mean?"

He went on, "You are probably like me. I learn by seeing and touching." Then he said, "Find the base hot plant." He continued, "Go see the boilers, and if possible, touch them." Then he repeated what my SWOS instructor had stated, "The guys in your class are getting better grades because they have seen the materials before, some as recently as six months ago. Hearing him repeat what my instructor was saying helped me to understand what I was experiencing.

In hindsight, I wish I had received my brother's advice earlier. By the time he and I began our twice weekly talks, I had lost nearly twenty pounds and was in danger.

At the end of the VOGELSANG orientation tour, I went back to SWOS and graduated. Soon after, I received orders to the USS JOHN F. KENNEDY (CV67) and was promoted to Lieutenant Junior Grade.

After SWOS, and with orders to KENNEDY in hand, I fully appreciated the Latin phrase, Vine Vidi Vicci (I came, I saw, I conquered). In my mind, I had succeeded beyond my wildest dreams.

(*For years I thought I had been granted a special consideration when I was sent to the VOGELSANG. I have since learned that I was just one of many minority officers at SWOS who had difficulty with engineering and navigation classes.*

As I was going through my "ordeal," the Navy was apparently accepting that there might be differences in the quality of some officer source programs. Soon after my situation, shipboard orientation became a normal part of many junior officer's post OCS, ROTC and pre-SWOS experiences.)

Chapter 3

USS JOHN F. KENNEDY (CV-67)

Fresh in my mind the morning I reported aboard KENNEDY in May 1978, were several things that made me immensely proud. My assignment to the KENNEDY was the culmination of a major personal journey. As I approached the massive man-o-war, tied up at Pier 12, Navy Operations Base, Norfolk, VA, I recalled many had told me that becoming a naval officer was one of the more difficult things one could accomplish. Yet I had done it.

As I walked up the brow of KENNEDY, stopped, saluted, and asked for permission to come aboard, my mind went back to when I first reported aboard a Navy vessel. In January 1966, fresh out of bootcamp, I reported aboard the USS DOUGLAS H. FOXX (DD-779). The ship was in dry dock at Portsmouth Naval Shipyard. It was sitting on blocks, covered in red lead, and shore power lines coming out of all openings. I was appalled.

KENNEDY, tied up at Pier 12, Naval Operations Base, Norfolk, VA, looked majestic and awesome. Even without the air-wing onboard, KENNEDY looked powerful and had the feel of a man-o-war. To play on an old Navy saying, KENNEDY was haze gray, and looked ready to get under way. By contrast, FOXX set me in mind of a person on life-support, her best days behind her.

I mentioned earlier, at SWOS I was asked often, "What was your source program?" Meaning? Where did you go through basic officer training? Another way of putting it, "Did you go to OCS, ROTC, or the Academy?" My answer was always, Direct Appointment. That answer usually prompted, another, "How did you make it through SWOS without a "source program?" During my KENNEDY check-in, I was made to understand the difficulty of that accomplishment which made me even more proud of being a member of the crew.

Onboard Kennedy, other unrestricted line (URL) officers and I stood bridge, engineering, and com watches. So, I got to put into practice what I had learned at SWOS. However, KENNEDY, being a carrier or bird farm, was not the place for a URL to excel. As a result, there were other areas where one could pursue a restricted line specialty.

When I arrived on board, I was assigned to the Administration Department. I later found that assignment had come out of my CT and Radio/Television experience. I had been selected because the admin officer, Lieutenant Howard Wallace, had wanted someone to run the onboard television, radio, and newspaper. That fact was made known to me during my initial meeting with the executive officer (XO), Commander Paul Feran, USN. During our talk, he remarked about my road from CT2 to LTJG.

Specifically, he said, "I have met many men who have done commendable things. I have never met anyone who has gone through what you must have just to become an unrestricted line officer." He concluded, "You should be proud of your accomplishment!" Until the XO stated it, I had not really given it much thought. If it had ended there, I would have walked away feeling appreciated. But then I had my one on one with LT Howard Wallace, USN, the ship's admin officer.

He was straight forward and honest in my assignment and his assessment of the division.

I was told "You will be assigned to X-2 Division as the assistant public affairs/media officer. You will have responsibility for all public affairs, as well as the ship's internal radio and television operations, the ship's newspaper, *Bird Farm News*, and the ship's post office."

Then Wallace said, "At sea, there is nothing more important to the morale of the ship's personnel than the recorded canned television programs, daily live newscasts, reports on activities around the ship, and the live programs featuring the command master chief, the executive officer, commanding officer, and the embarked Admiral." He went on, "You will have working for you a chief journalist (JO), a postal clerk chief (PC), a first class JO, an interior communications tech (IC), and ten strikers who have absolutely no experience whatsoever."

In the meeting with Wallace and me was Lieutenant Greg

Stidom, the current public affairs officer, who let me know he was in receipt of orders and would be turning over to me as soon as possible. With that, Wallace said to me, "I hope you are prepared to work your ass off!" What else could I say, other than, "Yes sir!"

After that meeting I met the rest of the division.

Chief Journalist Leonard Johnson was "a brother" from New York City. He had the demeanor of a person who was experienced and knew it. He let me know that he was planning to retire as soon as we completed our upcoming Mediterranean Cruise. His assessment was, "I can make you and the division a star in the Atlantic." He concluded with, "My goal is for the KENNEDY to earn the Golden Mike before I head off into retirement."

At the time, I had not known of that public affairs award. I later learned it was awarded to the ship in the Atlantic Fleet with the best overall Public Affairs program.

Next, I met Chief Ulysses "Pete" Woodley. Woodley, like Johnson, was an African American. However, they were opposites. While Johnson was braggadocios, Woodley was low key in temperament and demeanor. He struck me as being like most of the postal workers I knew in civilian life. He knew his trade and was focused on training his people and getting the work done. I was impressed when I learned he had made chief in less than ten years.

Our first conversation took place in a passageway outside the ship's post office. When I questioned him about that, he simply said, "Sir, postal regulations only allow postal employees inside the postal handling area." He went on, "While you are my division officer, you are not cleared to be in the space." I took it at face value and never pushed him on it.

When Johnson came back to meet me, he said, "Sir, did Pete let you inside the post office?" Before I could respond, Johnson said, "I hope you don't feel slighted. Pete has even challenged the skipper about entering the post office." Concluding, "He is a real stickler about postal regulations." I had no response.

Next, I met Petty Officer Jamie McCaine. I later learned that he and Johnson had been at loggerheads from the beginning. Johnson knew newspapers and writing. McCaine knew television and interior communications. Johnson could have cared less about either. Writing was his thing. And rather than stay out of each other's way, they clashed. I knew I would have to separate the two of them. McCaine would help me to make the decision. During the work-up for the upcoming Med Cruise, rather than continue to clash with Johnson, McCaine asked to be transferred to the Master at Arms Force.

Next, I met JO2 John Fahnley. The JO2 idolized Johnson. I later learned that it was Johnson who reviewed and edited nearly all Fahnley's writing. Also, like Johnson, he had ambitions of winning the Golden Mike. Later, during the Med Cruise, I would learn Fahnley had a flair for on-air TV work, which could play a part in winning the Golden Mike.

Then there was Petty Officer First Class David Bagley. He and the other IC techs would end up saving me when it came to television production and interior radio broadcasts.

My meeting with the strikers was interesting. Most were in the Navy because they had nothing else to do and often had no idea what they wanted to do. As a result, they often ended up in jobs that involved working on the flight deck. One experience with the flight deck during air operations usually led to an awakening.

The world of the flight deck, vultures' row, and the fantail, and all its essential parts can offer great views of the sea. It is a place where planes take off and land, and bombs and missiles are carried to parked aircraft. It is loud and crowded.

The flight deck, hangar bays, and fantail are hectic places that can be extremely dangerous. One can be blown over the side or sucked into a jet engine, not to mention the ever present danger of fire or an explosion.

Working on the flight deck requires one to be always physically and mentally in condition and alert. The slightest mistake can result in an accident or death. To sum it up, working on the flight deck is one of the most dangerous jobs in the world.

Nearly all my strikers had wound up in X-2 because they had the experience of flight operations and dreaded life on the flight deck. Once we got underway for the Med, the mere threat of sending one to the flight deck was usually enough to motivate even the worst of the worst sailors to straighten up.

By contrast, life "below decks" on a carrier can be likened to life in a big city, though somewhat crowded. The carrier has many of the big city amenities including choices of places to eat, doctors, dentists, barbershop, etc. When the strikers got used to life "below decks," they hardly ever wanted to return to the flight deck.

Once the ship got under way for the Med and with LT Stidom gone, I became the division officer. I could hardly believe my good fortune. In less than two months, I was being given my own TV/Radio and newspaper operation. I intended to take full advantage of the opportunity! And Chief Johnson and I began to focus on earning the Golden Mike.

Our first task was to assess the talent working for us. In his opinion, we had some of the most talented of the JOs and strikers if they were given the opportunity. Part of "giving them the opportunity" was to insist we stop calling them seamen and strikers. Instead, Johnson asked that they refer to each other by their civilian media titles. If they worked primarily on air, they were to be called reporters, field reporters, or anchors. If they worked on the newspaper, they were to be referred to as writers, editors, or print/layout artist. I thought it a bit much, but went along with Johnson's ideas.

Next, we focused on enforcing a dress code. As Johnson put it, "I want people on the ship to know you work in the TV Studio (X-2 division). Bellbottoms or dungarees were fine, but they must be clean and pressed," he told them. Then he and I focused on "on-air" presence.

Time permitting, before a sailor did an on-air presentation, the individual was critiqued for presentation, appearance, and articulation. Most did not like the idea until they began realizing that some were creating a following among the ship's company.

Next, the chief and I set up a meeting with Lt Wallace, the admin officer. The purpose of the meeting was to ask for funds to purchase special WJFK blazers. I reluctantly went along believing Wallace would say "No!"

When we met, Wallace's first question was, "What will it do for our sailors?" Johnson was prepared.

He answered, "It will set them apart from the other divisions." He continued, "It will make WJFK distinguishable from other shipboard TV stations."

Wallace laughed. Then Johnson added, "It will set us apart when we do our submission for the Golden Mike Award." Wallace stopped laughing and said, "I'll see."

We were given the funds to purchase the blazers which were used exclusively during "remote feeds" and in studio live feeds. The blazers were a hit with the crew. As one sailor put it, "It almost made me forget we were watching television on a boat." That comment led to the recrafting of the studio set.

One afternoon, I mentioned to Chief Johnson how easily we could build a background for the studio. We tasked the sailors with putting together a set made of cardboard and scraps from around the ship. It even included a window. Experimenting with back lighting, we were able to mimic some hours of the day.

Most saw the set design as fun and games. Then one afternoon, a group of the sailors built a window frame and brought it into the studio. Then they added curtains and a fake plant. I thought it a bit hokey until Chief Johnson told me that several of his fellow chiefs wanted to know how the TV studio managed to have a window when no place else on the ship had one. I have no idea how he explained that away.

Knowing that some of the on-air members of the unit were developing a following, we began seeking informal feedback from the crew on which "talent" they preferred. This competition helped to get some of the sailors to become more serious about what we were trying to do. The talent competition took on new meaning the first time we replaced an on-air personality because of lousy feedback from crewmembers.

With the studio designed and the beginnings of sorting out our talent, we turned our attention to the various canned products received from Armed Forces Radio and TV Services (AFRTS); a-farts for short. The only thing we found to "enhance" the many canned products sent our way was to toy with the "intro" for the programs we received. The best of the intros was the brainchild of Journalist Second Class (JO2) John Fahnley.

Fahnley was from upstate New York and loved gambling. At the beginning of our deployment to the Mediterranean, Fahnley brought the list of programs we would be receiving to Chief Johnson and me. Among them were your usual comedies, talk shows, and the entire NFL line-up of preseason and season games.

Fahnley knew how popular the football games were and

wanted to add something to them to make them more entertaining. His idea was the creation of a character dubbed "the Bookie!"

My initial reaction was to think we can't promote gambling in the Navy. After some discussion, it was determined that you can't promote gambling on games that had already been decided. By the time we aired the games, most in communications knew the outcome because sports and news often made up a goodly portion of the daily radio feed from the Navy communications station to ships at sea. So Fahnley was allowed to become "the Bookie."

When Fahnley became the "Bookie," he took on an entirely different persona. His voice changed. He wore blackened sunglasses, a black knit sailor's watch cap, and he completed the outfit with a heavy mackinaw topcoat. When the lights on the set were darkened, he projected the caricature of what one might imagine what the image of a bookie in a darkened room would be. He honestly looked like someone ready to take your bets (and money). But we still had to sell it to the command.

Fahnley had the answer for that too! "Let me do a preview of it for the admin officer and we can ask him to run it up the chain." He went on, "You liked it, he may like it too!"

We took the idea to LT Wallace. He loved it and took it to the XO, Commander Feran, who briefed the commanding officer, Captain Jerry O. Tuttle, who approved it immediately with the caveat that it "better never promote gambling." And so, "the show went on." Over time, Fahnley became a mini celebrity among crewmembers.

In fact, his depiction was so realistic that after the first times of airing the program, we began running disclaimers emphasizing the show was for entertainment and not betting. In his monologue, he explained that while the scores of the games were important, the play of the individual players was just as important. So, he dialogued about individual players and their skills, or lack thereof.

I thought solving the programming issue would put the unit on easy street. It did not. One of the most challenging of tasks the unit had to work with was the complaints of a lack of "service" in some berthing areas.

When called upon to investigate the issue, Bagley and his team of Interior Communications techs assured me that all berthing compartments had television and radio feeds. Upon further investigation, it was discovered that a handful of "ingenious" sailors were interrupting the signal and diverting it into their individual bunks. Those interruptions were degrading the signal downline. The signal was the least of our potential problems. If the problem was not corrected, it carried the potential of shock or electrocution for those who hijacked the signal.

To resolve the issue, the executive officer made looking for illegal feeds an item to be addressed during berthing inspections. The inspections were a success. However, in weeding out the illegal feeds, some compartments lost signal entirely. To resolve the problem, some berthing compartments had to be completely rewired.

Port Briefs were also the responsibility of the division. To put together a port brief required either the PAO or senior

JO to fly off the ship on the Carrier Onboard Delivery (COD) a day or two prior to the ship's arrival in port.

The COD's primary purpose is to ferry personnel, mail, supplies, and high-priority cargo, such as replacement parts, from shore bases to the aircraft carrier at sea.

The production of the briefs was straight forward and simple. The best video camera operator working with a still photographer and reporter would then attempt to bring to life the paper tour materials provided to the ship by a variety of sources including embassy personnel and host country tourism. The end-product was akin to a travelogue of restaurants, hotels and other sites and places to visit.

Senior staff were generally pleased with the end product. However, not so much among the average sailor. The reason? Crewmembers, particularly some junior officers, began criticizing them as "travelogues" of places not to go.

Often, they criticized them as being too puritanical, i.e., they rarely included entertainment sites like bars.

When run, the briefs usually began with a segment that featured the embarked admiral, the commanding officer, executive officer, and the command master chief or the PAO/media officer acting as on-camera talent. The segments usually consisted of in-studio talking heads interspersed between videos of local sites.

After the airing of the first couple of port briefs, Chief Johnson came up with the idea of designing a set with a table and chairs. This change involved using a "b" roll of local sites. (B-roll is a term used to describe secondary footage, often used as cutaway footage, to provide context and visual interest to help tell a story.) The combination of the in-studio set and the "B" roll made a difference to many crewmembers.

The changes made the de facto producers more aware of shot composition, camera angles, and multiple camera usages.

It also forced them to engage floor directors more actively. All those things had to be taught to the team because most had little or no television production experience. The in-studio changes also necessitated a certain amount to "training" for the principles too.

The first time I asked some of the principles (senior officers) to come to the studio for a pre-shoot run through, I was accused of wasting their time. To get around that, at the suggestion of Chief Johnson, we did our first "run-through" training with the command master chief. He was eager to help his fellow chief. He got it. And, as the saying goes, "it was a piece of cake." The master chief's experience got the senior officers to come onboard.

Some of the funnier moments of my tenure came during the trainings necessitated by the port brief "changes." One such moment took place during a shoot featuring the embarked Admiral, Rear Admiral Robert Schultz.

The off-ship shoot had gone well. What was needed to complete the product was to have the admiral come to the studio for the final production. AAll had gone well with the integration of in studio and on location videos. What was needed was to have the admiral stick around for a review.

The admiral was willing to hang out on the set. Anticipating that, I began reviewing while he was gathering his immediate staff to leave.

In my review, I noticed that in several shots, the admiral was seated wide-legged and unknowingly providing obvious crotch shots. Without thinking, I shouted to no particular person, "Don't let the admiral leave! Someone should have told him to shut his damned legs." Hearing what I had shouted, the admiral responded, "What did you say, mister."

The room fell silent as I stumbled over my words and replied, "Sir, what I meant was you should not have had your legs open during the shooting. I should have caught it and during our pre-shoot briefing addressed the issue as a form of non-verbal communications."

To my surprise, the admiral looked down at the floor and replied, "I guess you want me to shoot that scene again?" Sheepishly, I softly said, "Yes, sir." The admiral laughed. Then the rest of the team laughed.

Once the segment was reshot, the admiral came to me, shook his head, and laughed as he walked out, just barely audibly muttering, "Make sure that 'shut **your** damned legs' thing is not on tape!"

From then on, I began briefing the team and all prospective principles on media training basics: e.g.:

- If possible, ensure all principles have talking points, and go over them beforehand.
- Review potential questions and answers ahead of time. (To include possible negative questions.)

- Address non-verbal communications (facial expressions, seating postures, etc.) and possible negative impact.

During my tenure, the unit put together nine ports, " briefs each running an average of 15 minutes to a half hour. The ports visited were Rota, Malaga, Valencia, Barcelona, and Palma in Spain; Naples, Taranto, and Trieste in Italy; and Alexandria in Egypt. None were as funny as the *cojones* encounter with Admiral Schultz.

In addition to the broadcast side of media operations, as the PAO, I was also tasked with being assistant editor-in-chief of the ship's newspaper, *Bird Farm News (BFN)*.

At sea, BFN was printed and distributed daily to all divisions. Just like ashore, the admiral and the captain expected to have their copies of the paper on their breakfast table at 0600. To accomplish that, the division had a rotating shift of three sailors and either the chief or me as the senior editors. The team was strictly forbidden to just cut and paste articles from the Armed Forces Information Service wire service. The chief and I rigidly required those working on the paper to rewrite all articles, no matter how long or short the piece might be when received via the wire service

The best of the print journalist were Petty Officers Fahnley and Ray Strock. Prior to my arrival on KENNEDY, both had articles featured in All Hands Magazine. Fahnley was the writer and Strock was the lay-out print person.

In our quest to find stories unique to Kennedy, we featured stories about reenlistment in boilers, inter squadron sports events and Kennedy sailors reenlisting on-site at their workstations.

Personally, there were two stories that ran in BFN I am still proud of. Those stories featured KENNEDY sailors who went on a religious pilgrimage to the University of Al Azar and those sailors and Marines who re-roofed an orphanage just outside of Naples.

The University of Al Azar pilgrimage took place in November 1978 while KENNEDY was on a port visit to the Egyptian city of Alexandria, Egypt. The purpose of the trip was to introduce a few KENNEDY sailors who were considering converting to Islam to the practical applications of the religion in everyday life, dietary requirements, and the practice of the religion in a non-Islamic society.

The highlight of the tour came at the end when two of the men began the process of changing their names. The process was officially completed once the men returned to the states after the Med cruise.

The orphanage story appeared in the March 1979 addition of All Hands. The Family of Mary orphanage, just outside of Naples, was also the beneficiary of KENNEDY largesse. It received a new roof, constructed by sailors and marines from the ship. They also received new playground equipment and a cash donation of $2,000.

The official re-dedication of the facility took place on January 6, 1979, the feast of the Epiphany, the official last day of the Christmas cycle.

Of the many articles featured in BFN, the story of the

University of Al Azar pilgrimage came as a surprise to most senior officers. Before it was approved, Johnson and I had frequent conversations with the admin officer and the XO regarding the sailors. The men were also concerned because of the negative press often associated with the image of the Nation of Islam at the time. Outside of their small circle of friends, few knew they were trying to practice their religion.

To their credit, most KENNEDY senior officers were more interested in how they were maintaining Halal practices in an environment where few concessions were made for those with dietary restrictions.

It was only after the intervention of a career counselor, Aviation Ordinanceman First Class Toby Hoffler, that the matter was partially put to rest. When questioned about the men and their faith, it was Hoffler who answered the question, explaining, "The men had come to me seeking a way to practice their religion without attracting attention." He offered them the example of how the officers' mess operates.

In explaining it to the command, he asked, "Aren't officers and others allowed to draw some essential items from ship's stores and pay for others out of their pockets for "extras?" He continued, "That is what these men do."

Though not entirely accurate, the answer apparently ended the discussion because neither Johnson nor I heard anything else about it until about a month after the "special" tour to the University of Al Azar.

The trip to Al Azar took place around the time of the historic

Israeli-Egyptian Camp David accord. The story was carried in *Navy Times*, *Stars and Stripes*, the *US National Islamic Paper*, the **Bilalian News**, *Soundings*, and various regional US Papers. That story and the Naples orphanage story contributed immensely to the ship becoming a front runner for the 1979 Golden Mike award.

After about a year onboard KENNEDY, Captain Lowell Myers, who had relieved Captain Tuttle while we were in the Med, held a meeting with those aspiring to be Surface Warfare qualified. The meeting came about because many of the unrestricted line non-aviation junior officers complained because we were not getting enough underway bridge time.

During the meeting, Myers made it clear that his job as a carrier skipper was to qualify aviators. He finished by stating, "If you want surface qualifications, you should be on a surface ship." In response, I put my papers in to change my designator once again. This time I requested a change from unrestricted line surface warfare trainee to restricted line special duty public affairs.

When KENNEDY returned from the Med and moored alongside a snow-covered Pier 12 on Thursday, February 8, 1979, the goals that Chief Johnson and I had set for the unit had been met. By all accounts, the cruse had been a success for the Public Affairs, Internal Relations, and the Special Services unit.

Letters from home reiterated what I knew about KENNEDY based upon the articles that had been featured in, among others, *All Hands* and *Soundings*. In addition, soon after the ship's return, I learned that my request for a change of des-ignator had been approved by the command and forwarded to the Bureau of Naval Personnel.

The division was deep into putting the final changes on the *Ten Year JFK Cruise Book,* and the paperwork for the 1978-79 Golden Mike award had been submitted. Person-ally, I was proud, ready to go on leave and anxious to get home.

Usually, after a deployment, the airwing disembarks the day before the ship arrives in port. When KENNEDY arrived that February morning, cloud cover was bad, so the airwing could not fly off. Instead, the planes had to be craned off the ship so they could then taxi to Naval Station Norfolk, VA and fly to Oceana.

As I stood there on the bridge wing watching what was taking place, I had to laugh to myself. The planes looked like a grounded gaggle of geese waddling behind their leader to NAS Norfolk. Later, when I called home and told my wife about what had happened, she had no clue and saw nothing humorous in what I was trying to explain.

I left Norfolk on Saturday, February 10, 1979. That evening, my happiness turned to sadness. I learned that my mother, Grace Smallwood Collins, had been diagnosed with breast cancer just after the ship left for the Med the year before. She had less than a year of life remaining. I returned to Norfolk with a heavy heart and to a ship beginning an extended yard period. And, during my final year on KENNEDY, I came to understand and appreciate the saying "Sailors belong on ships, and ships belong at sea!"

Yard periods are probably the most hated yet necessary periods in any sailor's life. For me on the KENNEDY, it was particularly stressful because of my mother's terminal illness.

Once we pulled into the Portsmouth Naval Shipyard, berthing was near impossible. Junior Officer state rooms were being reworked. Those with families in the Tidewater area became commuters. Those who did not, were hot racking it nearly every night. I chose to move off the ship.

The chief and I struggled with keeping up with the men. While the radio station never went down for repairs, the TV studio was another matter. Upgrades and repairs were being done to all the electronic equipment and that included the TV station. We were able to continue producing the *Bird Farm News*, though the stories were not as interesting. During that period, we put the final additions to the *1977-1978 Ten Year Cruise Book*, and had it confirmed that the PAO shop had indeed been the recipient of the Golden Mike Award for the period of the cruise.

In port, alcohol, insubordination, missing watches, and un-authorized absences became big problems. The result being I found myself attending more Captain's Masts than I had ever thought possible. In one notable instance, a seaman ap-prentice had been accused of theft. The matter was referred to captain's mast.

Masts were straight forward and took less than twenty minutes. At that one particular mast, the accused was ar-gumentative and borderline disrespectful. To the surprise of all, the captain allowed him to rant on.

At the end of the man's statement, the captain pronounced, "I find you guilty as charged." Then proceeded to sentence him to seven days restriction, forfeiture of a half month's pay, and restitution for the theft. As the accused and others were filing out, the sailor was heard to mumble, "You can kiss my ass!"

Immediately, the marine present stepped forward. But the captain stopped him and asked, "Did you tell me to kiss your ass?" The sailor did not respond.

Without missing a beat, the captain said, "No man tells me to kiss his ass with his pants on." He continued, "Drop your trousers!" Stunned, the sailor did as he was told. Then the captain said, "Fold your pants and drape them across your right arm." Again, the sailor did as he was told. You could see from his crimson face that he had been humbled and wanted to apologize.

As we paraded out of the captain's office, you could hear a pin drop. The faces in the passageway expressed utter disbelief. No amount of explaining stilled the resulting rumors that spread about the sailor leaving captain's mast dressed in his cracker jack jumper, skivvy shorts, shoes, and socks. Fortunately for him, the XO was given the "privilege" of dealing with the obvious insubordinate remark. The young man was never again a problem while I was onboard Kennedy.

During the yard period, personnel problems paled in comparison to other issues such as fires.

In February, just three days after the carrier's return, a fire broke out aft on the 03 level in a living compartment. The fire was put out within an hour. It was later determined to have been caused by leaking steam igniting flammable materials, for me, it was an omen.

On 6 March 1979, KENNEDY spent the day offloading conventional ordnance. On 19 March, the ship moved to dry dock number 8, Norfolk Naval Shipyard, for her major overhaul.

During the ensuing yard period, among other things:

- The ship's tactical support center was redesignated as an anti-submarine warfare module.
- The NATO *Sea Sparrow* missile system replaced all three Basic Point Defense Missile System launchers and fire control directors.
- Ship's radars were either updated or changed.
- Carrier air traffic control was improved with automatic data readouts.
- Even the food service, air conditioning and laundry facilities were updated.

On 9 April, the ship experienced a series of fires set by an unknown arsonist. *John F. Kennedy* responded quickly and minimized the damage to only thirty-eight compartments during six hours' work at general quarters.

Unfortunately, thirty-four crewmembers were injured and a civilian shipyard worker, William L. Seward, lost his life in that fire.

On June 5, another series of arson incidents occurred. They were easily contained with no injuries and minor damages.

That series of fires, which started in an area off-limits to shipyard workers aroused new anger among crewmembers. A reward fund of $500 was created for information about the arson. To prevent a recurrence of fires, the ship doubled security watches.

While in the yards, most of the sailors spent one night a week aboard ship and the rest of the time in nearby barracks, to prevent a recurrence of fires.

Out of caution for my personal safety, I moved off the ship and rented a room in the home of one of my fellow junior officers.

On 14 July, the carrier shifted from dry dock to Pier 5 for the remainder of her yard work. There were no more fires during the rest of my tenure.

I spent the rest of 1979 and early 1980 introducing the Portsmouth community to its behemoth of a neighbor, USS JOHN F. KENNEDY. Through a variety of Navy and community requests, my office was responsible for arranging visits to the ship from community leaders, scouting scout units, veterans' groups, and senior citizens.

It was also during this period that I began to personally meet many African American sailors whom I came to realize were unrecognized or underappreciated Navy pioneers. Captain David Parham was the first of that group whom I had the opportunity to meet and spend time with.

The KENNEDY chaplain, Commander E.D. Ferguson, extended an invitation to lunch to Parham to introduce him to the skipper and the black officers in the ship's company.

As the PAO, it was my responsibility to pick him up and escort him to the ship. I relished the duty because it gave me time alone with the man many have come to recognize as the first black man to attain the rank of captain in the US Navy.

(An aside, when that kind of praise was mentioned in Parham's presence, he often corrected those paying him the compliment with the simple statement, "Robert Smalls was the first Black man promoted to captain in the Navy. He was given the command of the Confederate States Ship Planter and promoted to captain after he and a group of slaves sailed the Confederate States Ship out of Charleston Harbor and surrendered it to union forces.)

At the time, Captain Parham was the Chief Chaplain for Pastoral Care at Portsmouth Naval Hospital. The hospital was less than a ten-minute ride from the shipyard. When I went to meet him, I made it a point to park and go up to his office, optimizing my time with this historical figure.

During our ride together and later his lunch visit, I found him to be a genial man who was very much aware of his place in history. It was from Parham himself that I first heard the details of the full story of Dennis Nelson and the Golden Thirteen.

Hearing him reminded me of the conversations I had had with my mother concerning her work in the Officer Records Section at BUPERS in old Main Navy and later the Navy Annex.

As I recall her conversation, she stated, "Frequently, Navy

officers would come to the Records Section at the Navy Annex to review their personnel records, which were kept in a secure part of the office."

She would continue, "The security guard would call down to the section, speak to the supervisor, a white woman by the name of Vogle, who would then send an escort to meet the officer at the building's entrance."

"Escorts were assigned according to the race of the visiting officer. White women escorted white officers. And black women escorted non-white officers."

When I mentioned my mother's recollections of such visits, Captain Parham said, "Your mom must be proud of you."

And then with a subdued chuckle, he continued, "My how the Navy is changing." Adding finally, "Can you imagine what might happen in the future if things continue to change in the Navy at its current pace?"

Soon after Parham's visit, I was notified my request for change of designator had been approved and that I would be transferring to Navy Recruiting Area Five, Great Lakes Illinois, to assume duties as the Assistant Public Affairs Officer. Just before executing those orders, I was promoted to Lieutenant. I called home with the good news only to learn that my mother was literally on her death bed. I requested and was granted emergency leave. When I arrived home, my oldest brother Francis was there. Although retired by then, he had brought with him his senior chief's uniform. Three weeks before her passing, Momma got to see the two of us in uniform one last time.

The day after her funeral, I returned to Norfolk and began executing my new orders.

Chapter 4

Navy Recruiting Area Five

In March 1980, I detached from KENNEDY, en route to Recruiting Officer Management Orientation (ROMO). Upon completion of ROMO and general recruiting orientation, I reported to Commander, Navy Recruiting Area Five, Great Lakes, Illinois, as the Assistant Public Affairs Officer.

When I arrived in Great Lakes, I had the initial feeling that I was going to work in a world that was adhering to the promise of what Admiral Elmo Zumwalt had envisioned. My commanding officer, a woman, Captain Julia DiLorenzo, was well respected and at one time had been the second in command at the Navy Officer Candidate School (OCS), New Port, R.I. Her Newport background inspired confidence in me because I assumed that if she had been involved in helping create officers at OCS, then she must have known how to grow them once they were out in the fleet. She expressed those sentiments during our introductory meeting. My confidence in her was reinforced when she made me aware that at the Region level, I was entering a public affairs environment where minority officers were rarely seen. She also was the first to state, somewhat facetiously, "The public affairs community is known for eating its young!" I had no idea what she was referring to, though I would later learn.

The Navy Recruiting Area public affairs office consisted of four people. There was Lieutenant Drew Malcom, the PAO, me, the assistant PAO, Journalist First Class Robert Haggenson, and Photographers Mate First Class William Breyfoggle. It was through this team that Navy Recruiting Command Headquarters, Washington, DC, channeled funds for recruiting advertising. Aside from the annual Great Lakes Cruise warship visit, management and distribution of the advertising budget was the office's primary responsibility. However, because Area Five usually had more ports of call, the ship visit was always near the top of planning activities for the PAO staff. I learned that fact during my first few weeks in the office.

My first full month in the office was a flurry of activities, which included two major projects. The first was preparing for the port visit of the Great Lakes Cruise ship, *USS Robert Owens (DD827)*. It monopolized nearly all my time from June to August 1980. The office had responsibility for coordinating local governmental involvement, local media, and Navy recruiting advertising efforts in each of the ports the ship visited as well as briefing the ship as it transited those ports of the Great Lakes Region within Area Five. The ports included Chicago, Illinois; Milwaukee, Wisconsin; Green Bay, Wisconsin; and Duluth, Minnesota.

The second was traveling to the eight states and Navy Recruiting Districts (NRDs) that made up the Recruiting Area. The NRDs were Chicago, Il; Milwaukee, WI; Kansas City, MO; Kansas City, KS; Omaha, NE; Davenport, IO; Minneapolis, MN; and St. Louis, MO.

Of those, the office devoted resources and much time to the cities of Chicago, Milwaukee, and Minneapolis because each of those NRDs had much of the total of 150,000 or so visitors to the ship during its visit.

Amid this, I was introduced to the staff of the Navy Office of Information, (NAVINFO) Chicago. The office was headed by Captain Jack Martin, his deputy was Lieutenant Commander Charles Connor, and his assistant, Lieutenant Susan Hanson. The office had civilian administrative help, but had no other military personnel, in particular no journalist was assigned to it. Frequently, to assist them in their journalist needs, Drew would allow Haggenson to go to the NAVINFO to "help out."

The NAVINFO's responsibility was to keep the Chief of Information (CHINFO), Washington, DC informed of Midwest activities that might have public affairs impact on the Navy. They did this through direct liaison with local and regional mass media. A major component of their activities was appraising CHINFO on trends and potential problems relating to local media. While I was impressed with what they did, I noted to my captain that despite their proximity to Johnson Publications, publishers of Ebony and Jet Magazines, they had virtually no relationship with minority media. Like many in the military at that time, minority media was viewed as unimportant or marginal at best.

The visit of the OWENS went off and concluded without a hitch. Much of the success could be attributed to the experience of the naval reservists who came from Milwaukee.

The reservist team was made up of Lieutenant Commander Phil Volwrath, and Lieutenants Robert Germinaro and Maurice Wozniak from the Kenosha, Milwaukee area.

Phil Vollrath ran his own public relations firm and was known in the market in each of the cities visited. Germinaro was a long-haul trucking executive who knew distribution. And Maurice Wozniak was a reporter for the Milwaukee Sentinel. Their knowledge and civilian positions gave them the flexibility needed to successfully support the varied needs of the visiting warship.

The fact that the team lived in the Milwaukee area made it feasible to provide low cost or no cost Temporary Additional Duty orders to bring them onboard for the OWENS visit and future port visits. The Milwaukee naval reserve component welcomed the use of their people. It provided them a major event that supported the active duty Navy.

In her reports up the chain to recruiting command, Captain DiLorenzo always made it a point to express her appreciation for the support of the Milwaukee Naval Reserve Unit during the Great Lakes Cruise. No other units within Region received such accolades. On more than one occasion, she made it a point to make it known that she would seek their support as long as she was Commander of Navy Recruiting Area Five.

With the summer of 1980 turning to fall and the departure of the OWENS, the office got a real surprise. Drew Malcom, the Area PAO, received orders to Puerto Rico. His transfer came nearly a year earlier than what should have been his normal rotation.

Drew's numerical replacement was a new Public Affairs Officer, Lieutenant Karen Roach.

Like me, Karen was a direct appointee who had been commissioned based upon her experience as a civilian public affairs specialist. Unlike me, Karen had been commissioned as a Lieutenant while I was commissioned as an ensign. Also, unlike me, Karen had no prior military experience. And to add to the mix, her date of rank made her senior to me.

Once I learned that fact, I contacted the public affairs detailer, Commander Art Norton, and asked for guidance in the matter.

His curt response was, "Date of rank does not matter. You are the public affairs officer." He went on, "There should be no protocol issues, you are a lieutenant with enlisted experience, I expect you to manage any issues and ensure she is well trained!"

I took the matter to Captain DiLorenzo who assured me that what I received from Norton was typical of many male officers; that is, women should not be in the military. She concluded with, "There is a network of women here at Great Lakes who can help Karen if she needs it." She continued, "I can assure she will get professional and other help if she needs it." DiLorenzo's comments were reassuring. Karen reported aboard and about a month later Drew departed.

Before his departure, Drew introduced Karen to the staff at the NAVINFO. I was pleased to see her stepping into a relationship with the NAVINFO. I believed only good could come out of such a relationship.

After Drew's departure, Haggenson became more available for in-house projects while Karen became more immersed in NAVINFO related projects. Such a decision also grew out of NAVINFO beginning to recognize that Karen and I were unique in that no other Recruiting Region had a Black male and a white female officer team available to do local media interviews. Karen and I also liked the idea because it fit the minority representational narrative that the Navy was advocating at the time. We also liked it because Karen and I believed we epitomized the physical image Admiral Zumwalt had hoped would define his vision of a "new, more inclusive Navy."

At the time of Drew's departure, the office consisted of three other minority or female officers. They were an African American Officer Programs Recruiting Officer (OPO) Lieutenant Alfred Ford; a white female, Marketing Lieutenant Commander Sandy Regan; and an African American female, Minority Recruiting Officer (MORE) Lieutenant Lynn Vaughn.

All three had experience in Navy recruiting at the district level. Karen and I saw them as opportunities to expand the visibility of the Recruiting Area, especially in the minority recruiting markets of Chicago, St. Louis, Omaha, and Milwaukee. Navy Recruiting Command also noticed the uniqueness of the Region and began involving us in more of its marketing efforts.

Throughout 1981, Recruiting Command hosted recruiting conferences in Chicago, Milwaukee, Omaha, and St. Louis. Our office and Area Five Public Affairs played major roles in each. We were tasked with coordinating facilities, assisting in making hotel arrangements, identifying and acquiring Navy static displays, and post conference, assisting with the tracking of public affairs outcomes of those meetings.

Another unique thing about Recruiting Area Five was the existence of the Naval Reserve Construction Battalion Unit in Omaha, which assisted in acquiring and building static displays for conferences and public events. The unit constructed model ships, planes, and other static items that were otherwise hard to order. The demand for their work had to be tightly controlled because the costs of their projects came directly out of the Recruiting Area Five Public Affairs operating budget.

Late Fall 1981, the NRD Chicago OPO, Lieutenant Ike Owens, introduced me to Mr. Jesse Arbor a member of the Golden Thirteen. Although I had previously heard of Mr. Arbor and the class of regularly commissioned African American naval officers, I was pleased to meet him and hear his personal story. I was also aware of the 1978 meeting in Coronado, CA, where they had been given the name "Golden Thirteen." I was also very curious about meeting him because I could not understand why the Navy had not done more to honor them and use their story as an aid to be recruiting.

Mr. Arbor, Lieutenant Owens and I met at the McCormick Center just south of downtown Chicago. I was impressed by his size.

He was a big man with a self-assured, welcoming smile. He dressed like a man who knew how to be fashionable but not flashy. That is, although he did not have on a tie, he was wearing a suit and a vest, and highly polished shoes that had all been coordinated. How he was dressed told me he could have easily converted his seemingly relaxed appearance to a more formal one had the occasion dictated it. His handshake, though firm, was not overwhelming. After brief intros, Owens left the two of us.

Before leaving for the McCormick Place Convention Center, I had told the office where I was going and that I would be back around noon. I had not eaten and did not expect to until I returned to the office, so I offered to buy Mr. Arbor breakfast. He accepted and offered to lead me to a nearby place.

After a short drive, we found the diner; a storefront restaurant bar, which I later learned was a block or so from the cleaners Mr. Arbor operated. As he pulled into an open spot, I noticed there were no other parking spaces, so I had to circle the block.

When I returned, there was Mr. Arbor standing in the middle of the street motioning me to a space that happened to be adjacent to a fire hydrant. I objected. But then I noticed that standing next to him was a police officer, who was also motioning me to the same space. So, I parked.

As I got out, the police officer said, "If you are with Mr. Arbor, don't worry about getting a ticket." He continued, "Jesse is a friend of mine!" I smiled and followed Mr. Arbor into the store front.

Inside, he led me to a table at the back of the store. We sat down, and immediately a server, asked, "Mr. Arbor, what is your friend drinking." I responded, "Coffee with cream and sugar. And…" Before I could finish my sentence, Mr. Arbor cut me off saying, "What kind of sailor are you; I know you drink something stronger than that!" Thinking I would humor him, I said, "Hell, give me a rum and coke to go with that coffee!" Mr. Arbor laughed and said, "And, I will have my usual. And give us some scrambled eggs and hogshead cheese!"

I could hardly believe I sat there while he ordered hogshead cheese. I hate hogshead cheese.

When the order came, I had drunk one cup of coffee and a rum and coke. So, I ordered another, took a swig of the rum and coke, a heaped forkful of hogshead cheese and scrambled eggs, chewed fast and swallowed.

Jesse noticed, gave out a laugh and said, "You ain't from the south, are you boy?" Before I could answer, Mr. Arbor began telling me about his war experiences in the South Pacific and later at Great Lakes.

When I told him my mother had worked in officer records, he smiled and said, "I always wondered why I only saw colored women when I went to review my records." He went on, "I bet they were there just so we did not have to speak directly to white women."

Then we turned to his experience with Navy Recruiting District Chicago and the Navy Office of Information.

His response was simply, "If it were not for Lieutenant Owens and those guys at Glenview, there would be no involvement." He continued, "After the meeting in Coronado, we thought the Navy would do more with us."

By that time, I was on my third rum and coke. I blurted out, "The Navy owes you guys more than what you have received." I continued, "The Navy and the nation owes you a "Thank You!"

Mr. Arbor let out a big laugh and said, "Boy, you got an imagination!" He went on, "What do you think should be done." I responded, "How about a reunion at sea?" He shook his head and said, "In a pig's eye!" I had no other answer than, "You will see!"

I looked at my watch, realizing it was nearly 11 AM, and that it would take me an hour to get back, I stood up hurriedly, ordered a cup of coffee to go and said, "Mark my word, there will be a reunion at sea." Mr. Arbor said nothing.

Following Mr. Arbor's directions, I found my way back to the Dan Ryan Express Way. En route, I called the office and let Karen know that I might be late getting back. She asked how the meeting with Mr. Arbor went. My response, 'I don't know. But I promised him and the rest of the Golden Thirteen a reunion at sea! "She laughed and said, "What a hoot? And how do you propose to do that?"

When I got back to the office, Karen was waiting for me. She just sort of smiled and said, "The captain wants to see you. I told her what you told me." She and I went in.

In the office was the captain, Julia DiLorenzo, the executive officer, Grey Libby, Admin Officer, Chief Frank Phillips, Lieutenant Roach, and me.

Barely raising her head, the captain said, "Do you want to tell me what's going on?" Collecting my thoughts, I responded, "Yes, ma'am!" Then I told her the entire story of the encounter with Mr. Arbor, leaving out the parts about the hogshead cheese and rum and cokes.

Commander Libby cut in before the captain had a chance to react, saying, "You had no authority to promise anything like that." The captain, shaking her head, said, "You made the promise. Now make it happen."

Before I could respond, she continued, "First, call Jack Martin and tell him what you did." Without another word, she glanced up and said, "Go do it!"

Jack Martin was the NAVINFO commanding officer and Chuck Connor's boss. In the few encounters I had previously had with Captain Martin, I got what amounted to a barely tolerant acknowledgement of my presence. I called.

Captain Martin came on the phone and said, "I understand you have promised Jesse Arbor a reunion at sea? Is that true?" I responded, "Yes, Sir, but let me explain!" Before I could continue, he said, "What is there to explain?" Then to my surprise, he seemed to turn away from the phone, because his voice dropped and I could barely hear him when he said,

"I am giving you to Chuck for him to handle this!" Then there was a click, followed by Chuck's voice saying, "No one is interested in that story." He went on, Mr. Arbor has been pushing for recognition for that group for quite some time." Then he said, "I doubt anything will come of it, but let me know if you manage to pull it off." Then he hung up.

I reported to Captain DiLorenzo the gist of my brief conversation with the NAVINFO. She barely looked up and said, "It is on you. You made the promise!"

Back in the office, I told Karen what had transpired when I went back to the captain. She smiled and said, "You got your idea approved." Perplexed, I simply said, "Huh?"

Then Karen said, "Use your imagination. Did Captain DiLorenzo say 'No?'" I replied, "No, she did not!" "If she did not say, no! Then she implied, 'Yes.'"

By the time Karen and I had that conversation, it was nearing 5PM central time; 6pm eastern. Besides, I was tired. It had been a long day. So, I decided to call it quits and took the story of the day and my promise home to my wife, Margaret. She liked it.

The following morning, I got to work early. I sent separate emails to Lieutenants Ike Owens and Max Allen. The email to Ike was thanking him for introducing me to Mr. Arbor and recounting the "promise."

The email to Max told him of my idea, my encounter with NAVINFO, and asked for him to support the idea of a reunion at sea.

Later that day, Max called to let me know that his chain liked the idea. His boss, Commander Thom Wylde wanted me to put the proposed idea in writing. I did.

Soon, Wylde shared the idea with his boss, Captain Thompson, who asked for more detail.

Over the next few weeks, I sent letters detailing the Golden Thirteen's history, their meeting at Coronado, and the efforts to achieve recognition by the late Lieutenant Commander Dennis Nelson, before his death in 1979.

Throughout the fall of 1981, nothing was happening with the idea. Most had forgotten about it. Just after Christmas, I received a call from Lieutenant Joyce Zellweger, who collaborated with Max on Navy Recruiting Command Public Affairs staff.

Excitedly, she reported, "Max and I are working on getting the Golden Thirteen onboard an east coast aircraft carrier." She went on, "A carrier is being considered because of the age of the men and some having limited mobility." I could hardly believe my ears. I asked, "When?" She said, "We are looking at sometime in March or April." Continuing, "Max is working on that angle. He should be sending you a letter confirming the details." The call concluded with names of ships, among them was KENNEDY! I was ecstatic.

Karen had heard part of the conversation and taken off to tell the executive officer, Commander Libby. As I headed out the door to find Karen, I nearly ran over Commander Libby, who was coming to me. Before I could say anything, Libby said, "Let's talk."

I recapped the idea, the call with Recruiting Command PAO, the possible ships, and the potential dates for the cruise. As I finished my verbal report, Libby asked, "Has recruiting command committed to paying for this? You do not have that kind of money in your budget." I thought to myself, "What an inane question?" Rather than verbalize my thoughts, I said, "Why wouldn't recruiting command pay for it?" His reply, "You better make damned sure, Mister!"

January and February 1982 were a blur. Karen and I continued to do NRD visits, attend local recruiting meetings, and track the recruiting advertising budget. Word was beginning to filter out about what was about to happen. Among our most fervent supporters in what was now being called the at-sea reunion of the Golden Thirteen was Captain J. D. Firnback, Commanding Officer, Navy Recruiting District Chicago.

Firnback was one of the people who had been advocating for the Navy Public Affairs Office to do something with the Golden Thirteen, many of whom had ties to the Chicago area. For example, Jesse Arbor ran a business in the area and had worked as a Pullman car porter and as a doorman at the defunct Chicago Beach Hotel in Hyde Park; the late Reginald Goodwin became a successful attorney in the area after he left the Navy; John W. Reagan graduated from Lindblom High School in Englewood; Frank E. Sublett Jr. grew up in suburban Highland Park and Glencoe; and William White, a U.S. judge who graduated from Hyde Park High School and earned both a bachelors and a law degree from the University of Chicago.

Firnback's office was instrumental in helping to pull together the contact list used for the reunion and later gatherings of the men and others, who were known as the World War II Black Veterans of Great Lakes, hosted by my office after the cruise.

At the beginning of March, I was informed that funds had been approved for the trip. The trip was to take place the first or second week of April onboard the *USS KIDD (DDG 993)* out of Norfolk, VA. The ship was the lead ship in a class of destroyers that had been built for sale to the Iranian Navy at the time of the 1979 Iranian Revolution. The ship was undelivered, and consequently, the sale was cancelled and the ship turned over to the US Navy. Originally named *Kouroush*, the ship and others in its class which had been ordered by the Shah of Iran became known informally as the "Ayatollah class destroyers."

Invitational orders were cut and sent to the men. Soon after, I received my Temporary Additional Duty Orders to Norfolk.VA.

As I was leaving the office for Norfolk, Karen and I had a final meeting with Captain DiLorenzo and Commander Libby. I provided all copies of my agenda, orders, and contact information. My final act was to assure all that NAVINFO Chicago was up to speed on my agenda too.

I traveled to Norfolk and checked into the BOQ on Sunday, April 10. I decided to travel on Sunday to ensure I had time to deal with any last-minute issues, should they arise. Little did I know what was in store.

Monday morning, before leaving the BOQ, I called CNRC PAO to check in. I spoke to Max, who gave me the name and contact information for the LANTFLT PAO. I called, left my pager number, but got no call back. So around noon, I dropped by the office. The response I got made it plain that they did not have a lot of time for me.

I asked if they had received any of the messages from CNRC regarding the upcoming Golden Thirteen cruise. I was told the office had read something. Lieutenant Commander Kendal Pease concluded the conversation with "it sounds like a nice negro story! By the way, which Negro press do you expect to cover it?" Sarcastically, I said, "Your usual, ABC, NBC, CBS, and maybe UPI." I was then pointed in the direction of the staff Journalist, Petty Officer Second Class Jeff Katarski.

Katarski was pleased to see me because he had worked for me on the KENNEDY." Without further conversation, Katarski and I went to his office where he provided me assistance in identifying local media.

As the two of us headed to the back office, Katarski took me to meet the LANTFLT Admin Officer, Commander Howard Wallace. I was as surprised to see Wallace as Katarski was to see me. Wallace had been my boss on the KENNEDY. I then recapped for Wallace my purpose at LANTFLT, the story of the Golden Thirteen, and the upcoming cruise. He left and Katarski and I went to work drafting the press releases announcing the cruise.

Before leaving LANTFLT to distribute the press releases, I reached out to another acquaintance from the KENNEDY,

Lieutenant Commander Steve Pyles. I told Steve of my reception by Pease. He silently listened and then said, "Remember I told you the Tidewater Chapter of NNOA wants to do something for the men at Breezy Point "O" club?" I responded, "The best time will be late tomorrow after they have all arrived." Continuing, "The following day will be tight. I will have to get them to the helicopter pad to go out to the KIDD. And they will be at sea for three days."

After the call, Katarski and I revised the release to include the impromptu reception by NNOA at Breezy Point. The last thing I received from Katarski was a local media list. I looked at the list and found it incomplete. I thought of Chief Johnson, my journalist chief from KENNEDY. In the past, he had been knowledgeable of the Tidewater media market. In my search, I came across a number for another chief from KENNEDY, Postal Clerk Chief Pete Woodley. Though not a journalist, he knew the Tidewater area media market too! He met me as I was beginning my media rounds distributing press releases. At his suggestion, we initially went to the few print and electronic outlets that served the minority market. As we drove, I had an "aha" moment, partially borne out of frustration.

I turned to Chief Woodley and said, "I am subconsciously buying into that "minority media" crap thrown at me by the LANTFLT PAO." He laughed and said, "So what are you going to do?" I responded, "Let's go to all of the media outlets in the area."

For the next few hours, we drove all over Tidewater distributing press releases. One of the last stops in our rounds before returning to Norfolk was to the Christian Broadcasting Network (CBN). The rationale for that drop was more "why not?" rather than "what can they do?" Also, among our last stops were WAVY in Portsmouth, VA and the offices of the *Virginian Pilot Ledger Star* on Brambleton Street, Norfolk.

As I was walking out the front door at *The Pilot*, the gent I had handed the release to said, "This seems more like something that United Press International (UPI) wire service might like." He then directed me to a side entrance to the building and the stairwell UPI operated from. I handed the release to the receptionist who said, "Wow, this is interesting. I am glad you found me!" I thought nothing of it.

I dropped Chief Woodley off and headed back to the BOQ, watched some TV, and went to sleep early because I knew the next day would be busy. I figured I would have a leisurely morning before departing for base transportation and going out to the Norfolk Airport to meet the men.

The Thirteen, which now included Wesley Brown, the first African American Naval Academy graduate, were due to begin arriving just after noon. The next day came early.

At six o'clock the next morning, I was awakened by the sound of the ringing phone and a pounding on the front door of my BOQ room. Startled, I answered the phone first. It was Max. He was shouting, "Where are you?" My response? "Do you know what time it is?" His response was a curt, "Yes, I do." He went on, "What the hell did you do?" Without answering, I shouted, "Hold on, there is someone at the door."

I ran to the door to find a second-class petty officer standing there. Without any word of explanation, he said, "Admiral Train wants to see you." As he turned to leave, he continued, "I will be waiting out front in a car to take you to the admiral."

I went back to the phone and asked Max, "What in the hell is going on?" His response was, "That is why I am calling you. UPI picked up the story of the reunion. It is all over the wires here in Washington, and no one knew how to get a hold of you."

I interrupted him and said, "I gave the story to UPI last night. That is probably why Admiral Train has sent a driver for me." To which Max replied, "You shitting me!" I responded, "Getting dressed. Got to go. Will call you later."

When I got to Admiral Harry Train's office, I was ushered directly in. He was seated at a large wooden desk. With him were the PAO, Lieutenant Commander Kendal Pease, and the Admin Officer, Commander Howard Wallace.

When the admiral saw me, he got up, came around to the front of the desk, looked me in the eye, and said, "Are you Lieutenant Collins? I responded, "Yes, sir!" Without another word, he started into a tirade, "Who do you think you are? You came here for a reunion of naval officer pioneers on my base, and you did not think it was important to tell me?" "I had to find out about it on last night's television news?"

Before I could say anything else, he continued, "What is this NNOA thing? And why wasn't I invited to their reception at Breezy Point this evening?"

I began by explaining NNOA, which he was completely unfamiliar with. Then I told him the story of the reunion and the KIDD. Lastly, I told him about the reception, ending with, "Of course, sir, you and your staff are invited to the reception."

He then turned to Pease and said, "Did you know about this?" To which Pease replied, "Not entirely, sir!" Before he could continue, Wallace interrupted and said, "Sir, Lieutenant Collins was here yesterday and briefed us on the reunion." He went on, "Afterward, he and Katarski came by my office and told me everything, including the possibility of the reception." Wallace continued, "I assumed the PAO had informed you." Finally, Wallace concluded, "Sir, I have known Lieutenant Collins for a while. He was one of my division officers on KENNEDY. Katarski was in his unit when he was PAO on Kennedy." He concluded, "KENNEDY won its second Golden Mike Award as a result of Collins' leadership." With that, the admiral seemed satisfied and pleased, especially because he had his invitation to the Tidewater NNOA Reception for the Golden Thirteen.

As soon as I could, I called Max. I caught him as he was about to leave for Washington national airport for a mid-morning flight to Norfolk. Before I could tell him about the encounter with Admiral Train, he blurted out, "That is what I was trying to give you a heads-up on." He continued, "Folk have spoken to CHINFO and NAVINFO Chicago, and they have called your boss." He went on, "They are giving the impression that you were on some kind of rogue mission." Concluding, "Finally, Commander Wylde, my boss, had to step in and bring everyone up to speed."

At the end of my call with Max, I called Captain DiLorenzo, who seemed not to be upset with how things were going. As the call ended, I recall her saying, "Watch yourself, you have embarrassed some very powerful people!"

When I got to the airport, Max had arrived with Wesley Brown. They were talking to WAVY reporters camped out in front of the airport waiting for the rest of the Golden Thirteen. By two o'clock, all the men except Mr. John Reagan had landed. His flight from the West Coast was not expected to land before 4pm. So, we planned for a Navy car to pick him up and bring him to Breezy Point for the reception, scheduled to begin at 6pm. The men were taken to the BOQ at Navy Operating Base (NOB) Norfolk to freshen up. Most had expected to relax for the evening and go to the ship the next morning.

When it was mentioned that we were going to the "O club," most thought they were going for dinner only. On the bus, the men were told of the reception and the possible meeting with Admiral Train. None of us were prepared for what awaited us at the club.

A little after 6pm, the bus, now containing all the men and Mr. Reagan, pulled up to the club. At the entrance to the club were representatives from the local ABC, NBC, and CBS affiliates. Behind them, cheering, were the members of the NNOA Chapter, and various on-lookers. Among them, smiling broadly, were Admiral Train and other members of the LANTFLT staff, including Commander Wallace, and Lieutenant Commander Pease. In the revelry, I thought,

"Maybe the ruffled feathers have been soothed." The reception ended around 8PM. All retired to the BOQ.

Early the next morning I got a pager message from Karen. I called. For once, she seemed lost for words. In her excitement, I was able to gather that the stories about the Breezy Point reception and upcoming cruise had made the airwaves back in Chicago. She said, "The captain wanted you to know how pleased she is." I replied, "Great! Let's see how they play the cruise!" The call ended with, "I've got to run. We are taking the men to breakfast and then to the helicopter pad to go out to the ship!"

Things were going smoothly until just after breakfast. The men were used to eating breakfast and most meals leisurely. As a result, we found ourselves falling behind schedule. Time on site for lift off at Naval Air Station Norfolk was 0900. At 0830, the men were just finishing breakfast and had not begun boarding the bus. It was at that point that we encountered a major problem no one had fully planned for.

When the men were contacted about their capability to participate in a shipboard at-sea reunion, all but one had indicated they were physically capable of enduring the rigors of such a journey. The one who had indicated 'some' difficulty was Mr. Graham Martin. What an understatement.

Mr. Martin had terribly disfigured legs and painful knee injuries necessitating the use of a walker. They were the result of many years of playing and coaching football, both in the Navy and in civilian life. When the idea of the at-sea reunion originally surfaced, he had been one of the first to respond 'YES' to participating. Later, when asked about limitations due to his old injuries, his response was, "The cruise is too important. I can't let some old football injuries stop me!" And that was his attitude that morning and throughout the cruise. His mindset influenced the others. He was never left alone to any task throughout the shipboard reunion.

The men arrived onboard KIDD just before noon on April 12, 1982. From the flight deck, they were ushered to their shared staterooms and then to the wardroom for lunch with the commanding officer and officers of KIDD.

Commander William Flanagan, the ship's commanding officer was the KIDD's first skipper and proud of the vessel. During lunch, he briefed the men on the ship's history, its capabilities, the crew, and the events of the upcoming two to three days. The men were then given tours of the ship, starting first on the bridge. They witnessed Engineering Ship Qualification Tests. They toured the aft bridge, where they witnessed the close-in-weapons system demonstrated. They got to man the ship's helm. They toured the ship's Combat Information Center. They witnessed ship high speed runs, man overboard drills, and observed flight operations. It was flight operations on day two of the cruise that gave a boost to the at sea reunion experience and the entire story!

When the idea for the cruise was first suggested, the Navy had names and addresses for only eight of the known remaining Golden Thirteen members. Missing was Mr. James Hair. He had been lost in the massive mustering out that took place across all military services after World War II.

As providence would have it, on the evening of the night

of the Breezy Point Officer Club reception, a New York affiliate of one of the Norfolk stations carried the story and video of the upcoming cruise. Sitting at home in Hollis New York was James Hair, the missing member of the Golden Thirteen. Immediately, he called a local Navy Recruiting Station and identified himself as "One of them Golden Thirteen guys!"

Within a matter of hours, Navy Recruiting Command had verified his claim, cut him orders, and in less than a day, had him on a flight to Norfolk, on a Navy helicopter, and out to the KIDD. The evening of our second day at sea, Max and I got word via ship to shore radio of the find! We went to see Commander Flannigan, who had already received a call and gave us the information on Mr. Hair's onboarding. The next morning, at breakfast, the men were told. The reemergence of Mr. Hair injected a kind of magic into the cruise.

As word spread of Mr. Hair's expected arrival late on the afternoon of the second day at sea, the reunion cruise became the story of a reunion within a reunion. Some of the men were gathered on the bridge, others were in radio; still others had made their way to the helicopter hanger bay; all were anxiously awaiting word that the CH-46 *Sea Knight* was en route from Norfolk, approximately twenty minutes away. Finally, amid a lot of laughter and plain old disbelief, the helo landed and out of the hangar bay walked Mr. Hair.

All Hands Magazine of August 1982 reported the moment as follows: *"an exuberant group overwhelms James Hair with hugs and back slaps. "Take his helmet off," one shouts. "See if he still has any of his hair left." The protective gear is removed* *with a roar of laughter. The group sees that nearly four decades had left their mark -Hair had lost his hair!"*

The rest of day two at sea was spent reminiscing about how the Navy was, how they had changed, and what their presence on the KIDD might mean to the Navy.

The morning of the third day at sea saw the men still in a very upbeat mood. However, the realization that the cruise would be ending was beginning to set in. As they gathered their belongings, which now included USS KIDD ball caps, jackets and other memorabilia, many of the men wanted to call home to give personal accounts of the reunion and plan for airport pickups at home. The request for such calls was put to Captain Flanigan. Almost immediately, the captain turned down their request. A few feathers were ruffled, but most accepted the turn down without need for an explanation.

Late afternoon, the group departed KIDD via helicopter and returned to Norfolk to begin preparing for what they assumed would be an early Friday morning departure for home.

The next morning, the bus arrived to pick us up around 7AM. The men ate breakfast, gathered their belongings, checked out of their rooms, and placed their belongings on the bus in anticipation of departures for Norfolk Airport and the first flights, due to depart around 10:30AM.

The men boarded the bus for the airport, just after 9AM, only to be told there would be a delay. Some of them began to ask, "What the hell is going on?" Others threatened to buy personal tickets to their destinations and forego using

Navy paid-for tickets. Lieutenant Allen and I tried to calm them. Finally, we were able to get them to settle down and announced, "You are being held here because we received word that Recruiting Command wants all of you to come to Washington." That is why Captain Flanigan would not let you call home from the ship.

That explanation only prompted more questions, "Why?" "Who is going to tell our families?" In all honesty, at the time, we did not have an answer to any of those questions.

Begrudgingly, the men went to the airport.

When we got there, some of the men began demanding more information about the "why" of going to Washington. As we gathered them at the Eastern Airlines ticket counter, we finally got word from Washington that the Secretary of the Navy, John Lehman, and possibly President Ronald Reagan wanted to meet the men. That calmed the group down.

However, no sooner had that issue been resolved than we were presented with getting the group on a single flight to DC. The airline decided to hold a flight for the men. Problem? The departure gate was on the opposite side of the airport and the flight was scheduled to leave within the hour. It took nearly 45 minutes to gather the men and their bags and get them to the departure gate.

When the men finally boarded, the flight was already twenty-five minutes late departing. Flight time from Norfolk Airport to Washington, DC, National Airport is less than a half hour from wheels up to touchdown.

As the men boarded, we could visibly see that their fellow

travelers were not happy. Once the last of the Golden Thirteen was seated, the pilot was told who they were. Immediately, he went on the plane's intercom and made the following announcement. "Good Morning, ladies and gentlemen, Eastern Airlines thanks you for your patience during our delay this morning."

He went on, "The reason for our delay is that we have traveling with us some special men. They are on the way to Washington to meet with the President." Finally, he concluded with, "These men are known as the Golden Thirteen. They were the nation's first African Americans to be commissioned as regular officers in the United States Navy. Your patience and understanding is appreciated because you are helping them to conclude a long overdue historical honor." When the announcement concluded, a cheer went up from throughout the plane.

As we taxied down the runway, some of the Golden Thirteen wept. Others just simply smiled. All were nearly as exuberant as they had been two days earlier when they were reunited with Mr. Hair.

When the plane landed, the other passengers stood back and let the men deplane first. As they were leaving, those same fellow passengers cheered and shook each man's hands as they passed by.

In Washington, the men were taken by bus to the Clarendon hotel, close to the Pentagon. After getting all checked in, the group was told that plans had changed. Due to a scheduling conflict, they would not be going to the White House. Instead, they would be having lunch around 1PM with the

Secretary of Navy, Mr. John Lehman.

Onboard the bus for the short ride across the Pentagon Parking lot to the visitors' entrance, the level of incredulity increased when the men saw the crowds of visitors and media waiting for them.

Once we cleared Pentagon security, we were escorted to the Secretary's Office in the fourth-floor corridor of the "E" Ring. At the entrance, Secretary Lehman personally greeted each man, after which they were ushered into his private dining room. Lunch was not quite ready, so for the next half hour or so, they had Lehman to themselves.

Much of the time was spent talking about progress in race relations within the Navy, how impressed they were with the KIDD, and their reception onboard the Eastern Airlines flight en route to Washington, DC.

The time for the visit with Lehman had been scheduled for an hour. Around 2:30PM, nearly an hour and a half later, the men finally departed the Pentagon for the hotel. They assumed the rest of the day would be quiet.

As they broke into small groups, some had begun recounting the events of the past week. Others were anticipating calling home, to tell of their Pentagon visit. Little did they know there was one more impromptu event on the calendar.

While at lunch with the Secretary of the Navy, the Tidewater NNOA Chapter reached out to its DC counterpart. They, with the help of recruiting command, pulled together a farewell reception for the men. The reception began at 5PM and was attended by a variety of junior, mid-grade, and senior naval officers, including the Chief of Naval Operations, Admiral Thomas Hayward. The reception lasted well into the evening with the men signing autographs, exchanging phone numbers, and taking pictures with guests. As the evening ended, I found myself with Mr. Jesse Arbor.

As I escorted him to his room, and was about to say "good night," he smiled, patted me on the shoulder and said, "I have to say, you kept your promise!" I smiled, said nothing, and walked away, hardly believing what had transpired in just about a year and a half. By noon the next day, Saturday, April 17, 1982, all had boarded planes or otherwise departed for home. I went to visit my father, who still lived in DC. I remember his telling me how pleased my mother would have been to have seen the reunion. I left for Chicago and home to my family on Sunday

Monday morning, shortly after I arrived at work, Captain DiLorenzo came to my office, shook my hand, and congratulated me. She smiled and said, "Now that you have had some fun and a mini-vacation, let's get back to work!" And get back to work we did.

In the immediate months after the reunion of the Golden Thirteen, Area Five Public Affairs had three major events on its agenda. They were the coordination of the Navy Great Lakes Cruise warship visit, the fall swearing in of the Cardinal Company and participation of baseball legend Lou Brock, and the follow-on meeting of the World War Two Black Veterans of Great Lakes, which would now include local members of the Golden Thirteen. Each activity involved close interaction with the local recruiting districts, Navy

Recruiting Command, and port city civic and community leadership.

During my three-year tenure, the Great Lakes Cruise warship visits included two warships: one American and the other Canadian.

Ports visited included Oshawa, Ontario; Hamilton, Ontario; Buffalo, New York; Detroit, Michigan; Windsor, Ontario; Cleveland, Ohio, Toronto, Canada; Chicago, Milwaukee; and Duluth, Minnesota. The American warships paid visits to United States ports while the Canadians visited ports in Canada.

The port visits began in late May or early June when the ships entered the Great Lakes. Area Five ports included Duluth, Minnesota; Milwaukee, Wisconsin; and Chicago, Illinois. To ensure each port visit ran error free required either the Area PAO or the deputy, to meet and brief the ship's commanding officer in a port outside of Area Five. Frequently, that port was Cleveland, Ohio. The visit to Cleveland meant that my office was responsible for or involved in four port visits. And the busiest of the port visited was Chicago.

In my time in Area Five, the Chicago port visit always included the 4th of July Weekend and involved Navy Pier. As part of the port visit, participation often included other military units and bands like the Flight Demonstration Blue Angel Team, The Blue Angels, the Air Force Demonstration Team, The Thunderbird air shows, and the Army Golden Knights Jump demonstrations team as well as cook-offs, and drill team demonstrations by the U.S. Marine Corps, and other local and community activities.

The Navy ships for the visits during my tenure were *USS Robert Owens DD-827 (1980), USS William C. Lawe (DD763) (1981), USS William C. Lawe (DD763) (1982)* and the *USS EDSON (DD931) (1983).*

The purpose of the Port visits were to heighten Navy awareness and promote recruiting. Before the visit of the LAWE to Chicago in 1981, I generally shied away from certain activities. One of those activities was using the dial-a-sailor program to heighten visibility. However, recruiting headquarters liked the idea and pushed us to use it.

I was against the program because I saw it being fraught with potential problems such as the age-old images of the drunken sailor or the girl in every port. However, I was overruled. And the program moved forward.

The program was run during the LAWE port visit, July 13-16, 1981. It was advertised both in print and over the radio and TV with bold announcements to "invite a sailor to a picnic, backyard barbecue, or sightseeing." I cringed every time I heard it.

During the post port debrief for the LAWE, the ship's commanding officer, Captain Ted Kramer, pronounced the campaign a success. He based his comments on a Christian Science Monitor article dated July 13, 1981. The article, according to Kramer, reported that "The sailors and officers have managed hundreds of invitations... It has been fun and good for community relations." He went on "the crew's been invited on fishing and camping trips, pool parties, plane rides, skiing, and fancy restaurant dinners." https://www.csmonitor.com/1981/0713/071323.html. I still did not buy into the idea. And, just as I feared, it gave rise to another farfetched idea used in the following year's Great Lakes Cruise. That idea? Procure a goat and give it to the 1982 Great Lakes designated cruise ship to present to the city, which in turn was to give the goat to a local petting zoo. I was so embarrassed by my vocal opposition to the previous year's idea that I decided to keep my thoughts to myself.

On the surface, the goat giveaway (as I called it) sounded like something that was doable and less fraught with problems than dial-a-sailor. Besides, most knew that the goat was a symbol of the Naval Academy and hence the Navy.

In 1982, the ship was once again the USS LAWE. The commanding officer had changed. The new skipper was Commander Paul Murphy. When I met him during the pre-port brief, Cleveland, he greeted me and said, "Are you the guy who opposed last year's Dial-a-sailor program?" Before I could respond, he said, "I understand you guys have a pygmy goat for us this year!" Continuing, "I can't wait to see how successful that is going to play out!"

Commander Murphy physically encountered the goat the morning the ship arrived in Chicago, just minutes before he was to present it to Chicago Mayor Jane Byrne.

Lieutenant Roach had arranged to get Grant's Farm, a division of Anheuser-Busch, to donate the goat to the Navy. The goat was named Ms. Bud, in honor of Budweiser Beer. Three days before the LAWE's arrival, Lieutenant Roach and I were given permission to take a Navy thirteen-passenger van down to St. Louis to pick up Ms. Bud. To accommodate the goat, we had to remove all the passenger seats, procure tie down ropes to hold the goat, and paper for the floor of the van. Neither one of us had any idea about transporting live animals, least of all a goat.

The normal drive time from Great Lakes to St. Louis took about five hours. Once the goat was onboard, the return trip took twice that time. Why? It was only after an hour into the drive that we realized that paper on the floor of the van was a bad idea. Hay might have been better. We never took into consideration the need for ventilation. Goats poop and pee near nonstop.

We had no idea that "walking the goat" was not akin to walking a dog. In hindsight, Karen and I must have looked like idiots; two naval officers in white uniforms trying to walk a goat in a public park.

When we got back to Great Lakes, both Karen and I were goat weary and tired. The van stank to high heaven. And the goat was restless and barely controllable. Then add to all of that, because we arrived two hours after closing time for the local petting zoo, Lamb's Farm, which had agreed to board Ms. Bud for the night, I ended up having to take the goat to my house in Navy Housing. My kids loved it. However, my dog, a large black shepherd Labrador mix wanted none of it. So, the goat spent the night in the basement and the dog in the backyard. No one got any sleep that night with the dog barking and the goat baa-ing.

Around sun-up the next morning, before anyone could call the base police, I took Ms. Bud to Navy pier where she was housed in one of the out of the way public bathrooms.

The LAWE arrived on time at 8AM. After meeting Commander Murphy, Karen and I took him to the bathroom to meet Ms. Bud. The bathroom reeked. The goat was restless, uncontrollable, and hungry. Fortunately, I had stopped to get dry dog food for Ms. Bud.

When Murphy entered the bathroom, encountered the smelled, and saw the goat, he just stood there and shook his head and said, "Where is this damned thing going to stay until the major arrives?" Before anyone could answer, he completed his statement, "It damned sure ain't coming aboard my ship!"

We assured him Ms. Bud would stay in the bathroom until presentation time. The presentation was set for 11:30 a.m., after which the mayor would board the ship and have lunch with the commanding officer.

The mayor and her entourage arrived at exactly 11:30am. On the pier was Commander Murphy, the goat handler, Karen, and me. After greetings, the goat, which was being held on a six-foot dog's leash, was handed to Murphy, who in turn, handed the leash to Mayor Byrne. No sooner had the leash changed hands than Ms. Bud lurched forward, poked its head under the mayor's skirt and began to pull. The goat had a hold of the mayor's skirt and would not let go.

As others struggled against the goat, one of the mayor's security people stepped forward, gently wrapped his arms around the goat's neck, and began stroking it. Ms. Bud let go of the mayor's skirt. The mayor thanked Commander Murphy for the goat, handed the goat back to the Navy handler, and all went to lunch. In the meantime, Ms. Bud was ushered into the van and taken to Lambs Farm, its new home. And Murphy sent some sailors up to Lamb's Farm with the goat to make sure Ms. Bud had suitable accommodation. The mayor's people had little to say.

The press loved the story and featured it prominently, sans the part about the skirt.

After the departure of the LAWE, things in the office returned to its normal hectic pace of managing the recruiting area management budget and working with the eight recruiting districts, and hosting meetings of local civic groups. The groups included the Defense Advisory Committee on Women in the Services (DACOWITS), the World War II Black Veterans of Great Lakes, which now prominently featured the local Golden Thirteen members (Mr. Jesse Arbor, Judge Sylvester White, and Mr. Frank Sublet), as well as Lewis "Mummy" Williams, a member of the Golden Thirteen class that had not been commissioned, and SNC Nathaniel Hamilton (USN Ret.), organizer and founder of the Angel Drill Team, a local Navy oriented youth group. The normalcy of it all was quite boring compared to the Ms. Bud escapade.

Also part of our "normal routine" was the organizing, and hosting of Cardinal Baseball Team dignitaries who annually came to the graduation of the Recruit Cardinal Company. Throughout my time in Recruiting Area Five, baseball legend Lou Brock was prominent among the dignitaries.

The swearing in and the graduation of the Cardinal Company has been a long-standing tradition in St. Louis and Great Lakes Naval Training Center. Cardinal Company received its name from the St. Louis Cardinals Baseball team, who recruiting offices from the state together with Navy Talent Acquisition Group (NTAG) Mid-America and the St. Louis Navy League, have sponsored annually since 1958. The company is composed of recruits from Missouri, Kansas, central and southern Illinois, and a portion of Kentucky.

Brock was best known for stealing bases. He once held the major league records for most bases stolen in a single season and in a career. He led the National League (NL) in stolen bases for eight seasons. Brock was also a member of the 3,000-hit club.

During his visit to the base, before going over to Recruit Training Command and meeting the members of Cardinal Company, Area Five PAO hosted a reception for Brock and invited all base and local commands. Because of Brock's popularity, a sizeable portion of my office budget was set aside for that event and activities involving local publicity for the Cardinal Company. Often, Brock would regale the attendees with stories of his playing days. One story he loved to tell was the day he was late for a game, attempted to steal a base, and was tagged out.

According to Brock, "Before the first title series championship in 1964, I was traded from Chicago to St. Louis." He went on, "at the time, we couldn't afford to get an apartment in St. Louis." He continued, "I commuted from Chicago to St. Louis whenever we had a home game."

"On one of those trips, I was tired, so I pulled over on the highway to take a break and I fell asleep. When I woke up from my nap, I realized I was in danger of being late. We were fined $500 each time we were late." "So," he continued, "I drove from Chicago doing 90 miles per hour. Before making it to the ballpark, I got pulled over for speeding. I had to pay a $50 fine. I was let go and continued to the ballpark."

As the story goes, later that evening, during the game, the furthest thought from Brock's mind was that speeding ticket. But it was not the last time he would hear about the ticket.

Brock continued, "I came up to bat in the first inning that night and got a hit. Then I tried to steal second base and was called out. Naturally, I protested. And the umpire said, 'Awe, shut up! That's the second time today you have been caught speeding!'" Brock couldn't figure out how he knew what had happened.

The story continued, "for years, I tried to find out how the ump knew about my speeding on the way to the park." He concluded, "finally after nearly five years, I heard that the cop who had stopped me was a relative of the umpire." "After that," Brock said, "that particular ump and I became friends." I was never pulled over again!"

No matter how often Brock told that story, he always got a laugh.

As the summer of 1982 dawned on the office, we got word that Captain DiLorenzo would be relieved as Area Five Commanding Officer. At the time, I had been a public affairs officer since 1979 and approaching eligibility for promotion to Lieutenant Commander.

In reviewing my successes since becoming a public affairs officer, I felt confident of my chances for promotion from 03 to 04. Since leaving KENNEDY and reporting to Area Five, I had been the recipient of top 1% Fitness Reports and recommended for accelerated promotion.

Among accomplishments noted during that period was the role I played in KENNEDY's being awarded at least one Golden Mike Award. The Great Lakes Cruises of 1980, 81, and 82, had all garnered high praise and was reflected in each of my 1% fitness reports for those periods.

Other things noted in those same evaluations were my contributions to local recruiting efforts, best seen in the success of my office's involvement in the sponsorship of the World War II Black Veterans of Great Lakes, my office's active participation in the local Defense Advisory Committee on Women In the Services (DACOWITS) as well as sponsorship and promotion of public relations and community events around the visits of Baseball Great, Lou Brock.

All of these things paled by comparison to the nationwide media success of my idea for a reunion of the Golden Thirteen, although some in the Navy public affairs community had relegated it to being a "nice negro story," of little interest outside of the Black Community.

Despite such disparaging remarks, I honestly believed I had a better than average chance of being promoted to Lieutenant Commander if all those things were given an honest and fair assessment. How wrong I was.

Just after returning from the Golden Thirteen Cruise, I was approached by the Executive Officer, Commander Grey Libby. In a private conversation, he stated, "I want you to know that Captain DiLorenzo is extremely proud of your success with the cruise and is pleased with your overall work here in the area." I felt good. Then came the rest of it. "She has heard that others in DC who were involved with you in the cruise are being nominated for Navy Commendation Medals." He continued, "She believes you are deserving of recognition for your accomplishments. However, she has only one more NCM to award. And she is going to award it to our admin chief, Yeoman Frank Philips." He went on, "As you know, Chief Philips is retiring soon, after twenty years' service and has never been granted such an honor." The captain will note your role in the Golden Thirteen Cruise in your upcoming (fitness report) performance of duty. I could not believe my ears.

In July 1982, the staff was informed that Captain DiLorenzo had received orders. Not long after that, Libby came to me again to let me know that DiLorenzo wanted me to know that in her turnover, she had recommended that the incoming commanding officer, Captain B. Angus MacDonald, consider awarding me an NCM. My last fitness report from Captain DiLorenzo was a 1%, with a recommendation for accelerated advancement. I was disappointed, but I had no choice but to feel hopeful.

As DiLorenzo departed, so too did the executive officer, Grey Libby. He was replaced by a temporary active duty (TEMAC) officer named Commander John Dunning. He and I had met previously when he was the deputy at Navy

Recruiting District Omaha. I thought little of him while he was in Omaha. However, that would change once he came to Area. He reported aboard just before the change of command. His task was to work with my staff to ensure the change of command went smoothly. I soon learned he knew very little about change of command ceremonies. As a result, I questioned many of the tasks because they appeared to be outside the "normal" duties of a public affairs officer.

One such tasking relayed to me by Dunning from the incoming commanding officer was the acquiring of battle streamers for the American flag to be used at the change of command.

Streamers are decorations attached to military flags to recognize particular achievements or events of a military unit or service. They are attached to the headpiece of the assigned flag, the streamer often is an inscribed ribbon with the name and date denoting participation in a particular battle, military campaign, or theater of war. The ribbon's colors are chosen accordingly and frequently match an associated campaign medal or ribbon bar. They are physical manifestations of battle honors, though not all streamers are battle honors.

He was not sure what the new captain was seeking. I had an idea and passed the instruction along.

Today, there are over fifty tenant commands at Naval Station Great Lakes. In 1982, there were not nearly as many. My staff and I reached out to each one and none had an American Flag with battle streamers. From the tenant commands, we reached out to Navy commands in the region and eventually to Washington, DC. None had flags with streamers they were willing to lend. So finally, we went to flag makers, and none had streamers that would have arrived in time for the change of command. When I reported this to Commander Dunning, rather than break the news to the incoming commanding officer himself, he had me break the news to him. He was not pleased.

The irony in all of this is that once the change of command was over, I found that the captain and I were the only people on staff who knew exactly what he was desiring. Nonetheless, he stated, "As my public affairs officer, I would have expected you to have a handle on those kinds of things!" I did not know how to respond, so I said nothing.

Once the change of command was over, I approached the new skipper and inquired about the medal I had been assured Captain DiLorenzo would request he award me. His response was an abrupt, "You have not done anything for me. Why should I?" Then he went on, "From what I can see, Julia (DiLorenzo) was easy when it came to passing out awards." As he walked away, he said, "An award is based upon performance, not just because you occupy a position." I never brought it up again. In the meantime, I learned that Max, Joyce, and others at Navy Recruiting Command Headquarters, Washington, Public Affairs Office, had been nominated for NCM, though not all received them. Crestfallen, I turned my attention to the day-to-day activities of the office.

In the meantime, Captain MacDonald continued with his unusual tasking. For example, I was personally tasked with locating command silver service, and designing the quarter deck area display. The rest of the PAO staff was tasked with designing and ordering promotional buttons, pins, and a command plaque. When I questioned their utility in directly enabling recruiting, I was told that "rewarding productivity enhances production." When I mentioned that such things took away from the primary activities of the office, the captain dismissed my protestations as being akin to not being a team player.

Despite those tasks, the office managed to engage in managing the national Navy Recruiting Advertising office's local enlisted advertising delivery system (LEADS). We also continued to do local television appearances in support of recruiting efforts and designed and delivered training programs for the journalist and photographers who worked at the eight recruiting districts that made up Area Five.

Despite the "unusual projects," we took pride in continuing to support the various local communities unique to our office; groups like the local Golden Thirteen members, World War II Black Veterans of Great Lakes, and Defense Armed Services Advisory Committee for Women in the Services (DACAWITS). However, those groups that had not previously been on Captain McDonald's radar, soon fell under his scrutiny.

It began in a rather innocuous way. It began by his questioning in detail our appointment calendars. He wanted to know how each group contributed to the recruiting mission. The individual group's awareness of our being recruiters was never an acceptable explanation of the importance of the groups to the recruiting mission. He often replied "awareness is one thing. But show me how that translates into recruit numbers."

I had hoped that the new XO Commander Dunning would be an ally for me and my office. I soon became disavowed of that notion. As I mentioned, I had known Dunning before his arrival in Area Five. Dunning had been the Officer Programs Officer in Omaha, Nebraska. Like many on staff, he was a Temporary Active Duty (TEMAC) officer. His promotion and assuming of the position in Area Five was seen by many as a positive thing. During visits to Omaha, he was always hospitable and openly friendly. That demeanor continued even after he came to Area, where he became very friendly with Petty Officer Sherry Thompson and Journalist Chief Robert Haagenson.

I began to see he was not what he presented himself to be or what I had hoped for, an ally, when Captain MacDonald tasked me with many things that others in similar positions around the country defined to me as being outside of my job description. While Dunning was enthusiastic and appeared supportive, when it came to obtaining the battle streamer for the change of command flag, he did nothing to get the new captain's support for our endeavors. Instead, he only reported our failure to acquire the streamer. Later, he admitted that he did not know what the captain was seeking when he admitted to Lieutenant Roach, "I not about to admit to the captain that I did not know what he was seeking!

When I reported to Captain MacDonald that it was cost

prohibitive to purchase the streamer, he remarked, "I should have known you would come up with an excuse. Dunning told me you had no idea what I was seeking." When I approached Dunning about what the captain had said, his only comment was, "You are the PAO, you should have been able to beg, steal or borrow one."

After the change of command, I routinely went to Dunning regarding other taskings I had begun receiving from the captain. Among those things I took to Dunning was the captain's desire to purchase command China, designing promotion buttons, and designing a quarterdeck area for the entrance of Area Five spaces on the second floor of Building Three.

After some research, I found Command China was not something that any other recruiting area possessed. When I reported it to Dunning, he reported it to the captain, who demanded to talk to me. When Dunning and I went into the captain's office, MacDonald said to me, "Dunning says you think it is inappropriate for me to have command China!" Before I could respond, the captain said to me, "I don't care what you think. I want it. You find it and order it." As I was leaving, he concluded, "And it will come out of your office's budget."

Similar conversations followed when it came to designing and ordering command promotion buttons. I was ordered to acquire them, and pay for them out of PAO office operating budget.

Earlier I mentioned that Recruiting District Omaha had a Combat Battalion Reserve detachment in its area. Often, the unit would design static displays for use around the area and at other Navy commands. One afternoon, Dunning came to me and told me the captain wanted to see me. To my surprise, the captain had a blueprint of a design for a new quarterdeck area. Without much else said, the captain said, "Here Lieutenant, take this to those guys at the CB unit and have them build it." I did as I was ordered. When the CB unit received it, they immediately responded, "We have the materials to build it, but we don't have the budget for transporting it and installing it at Region." They concluded with the most important question, "Who is going to pay for it?"

When I reported to Dunning and the captain what the CBs said, I was told by MacDonald, "You were creative enough to find money for your meetings with those groups that have done little for us recruiting wise, I am sure you can come up with a way to pay for my new quarterdeck area!" As we walked away, Dunning said, "You can take that out of your budget too" Which I did.

It took nearly three weeks to build the new quarterdeck. Then it took a weekend to transport it to Region from Omaha. And another week to install it. To pay for the quarterdeck and its installation, we cut TDY orders for the six men who drove from Omaha to Great Lakes to install what some, including Dunning, were beginning to refer to as the "Altar." While these seemingly "little taskings" really perturbed me, it was the captain's mast on my journalist chief, Robert Haagenson, that really signaled to me that my office was in trouble.

Not long after receiving calls from Lieutenant Allen regarding the captain's many calls to the Chief of Information regarding me, Chief Haagenson was placed on report for being tardy. His tardiness was exacerbated by the fact that he had not called into the office that morning. When he did show up, word had circulated throughout the staff that he had been out the night before with Commander Dunning and Petty Officer Sherry Thompson. The problem was that it was not the first time Haagenson had done this.

Commander Dunning, Petty Officer Thompson and Chief Haagenson were known around the office as being close friends who often frequented the combined officers and enlisted club after work for dinner and drinks. That particular evening, Dunning and Thompson, who lived together, left Haagenson at the club by himself. The next day, no one could say definitively where Haagenson was. When he did show up for work, he was ushered into the captain's office and warned in no uncertain terms that he would be written up if he was tardy again. Note, I am using the term tardy.

Less than a month later, Haagenson went missing again. This time when he showed up a day or so later, instead of being chewed out, he found himself the object of an article 15. Despite overwhelming evidence that he had been with Dunning and Thompson the previous night, MacDonald was insistent on conducting Mast on Haagenson. As a result, the chief was fined a month's pay and the club was placed off limits to him.

When Lieutenant Roach and I approached Dunning regarding the matter, we were stunned by his reaction. He had nothing to say other than, "My friendship with Petty Officer Thompson has nothing to do with what happened to Haagenson. He was warned."

In coming down hard on Haagenson, Captain MacDonald was overlooking a clear violation of Article 134 — Fraternization, and imposing an article 15 punishment for what might have been at best intoxication. Neither Lieutenant Roach nor I could see the rationale in the captain's punishment or Dunning's comments. With Hogenson's punishment, we both began to accept the writing on the wall for the staff of Navy Recruiting Area Five Public Affairs.

At the time of the new captain's arrival, the officers on staff at Area Five consisted of Lieutenant Commander (LCDR) Sandy Reagan, Marketing Officer; Lieutenant Al Ford, Officer Programs/Aviation Officer; Lieutenant Lynn Vaughn, Minority Recruitment Officer (MORE); LCDR Roger Pinta, Supply; and Lieutenant Karen Roach, Assistant Public Affairs Officer; and me, Lieutenant Gerald Collins, Public Affairs. Not long after the change of command, Lieutenant Ford, a pilot, requested and was granted an early transfer. With Ford's departure, with the exception of me, all the other male officers on staff were white.

For those like the Enlisted and Officer Recruiting Officers, translating relationships into hard recruit numbers was an easy task. Their reports provided numbers that could be easily tracked and translated into bodies. For PAO and Marketing, it was more difficult to do this, but not impossible. To accomplish the task, we began asking marketing to attach an additional number to the enlistment package of each new recruit. By that simple act we could then begin translating our contributions into bodies and bodies into programs. It did not stop the scrutiny. Then Lieutenant Roach pointed out to me that there may be something else at play. She remarked, "Haven't you noticed that the white males are not scrutinized the way we are?" Frankly, until the time she made her comment, I had not thought of it. I was too busy trying to please the captain.

My opinion changed when I called Ford. In our brief conversation he told me he had experienced the same things I was. That is, Ford said, "I got a call from my detailer letting me know that the captain had begun calling and complaining about alleged inadequacies." He went on, "Without my asking, the detailer said, 'I am going to get you out of there before he damages your career!'" I could not believe that Ford, whom I thought was a friend, had not shared that information with me prior to his departure.

After Ford's departure, Captain McDonald's began being more open in his accusations about the PAO activities. Instead of asking, "What have you done to put someone in the Navy today?" He began asking, "What have you and your staff done to earn your pay today?" During one staff meeting, I instinctively replied, "Is that a real question?" He replied, "Do you think I am joking?" I replied, "No sir! I just wasn't prepared to answer such a question." Instead of moving on, he then went on to say, "From now on, I expect you to be prepared to give me a detailed verbal report on what you have done lately to put someone in the Navy." When the meeting was over, LT Roach pulled me aside and said, "He has asked similar questions of LCDR Regan, and

Lieutenant Vaughn." She continued, "He asked them such things in private meetings." She went on, "Now that Ford is gone, I guess he will turn his full public ire to us."

When I asked Regan and Vaughn about these remarks, they indicated that they had come up with a litany which seemed to answer the captain's question in the moment.

The litany they created went, "Today, I reviewed X document which is being used to recruit." As they put it, "the litany seemed to stop the questions, but by his facial expression, you could see it did not satisfy him."

In a later follow-up conversation with Ford, he said what neither Karen, Lynn nor Sandy would. That is, Ford said, "My detailer plainly stated, the man is a bigot." And, added, "I can leave you there, or I can transfer you to keep him from harming you further."

LT Roach and I went to see the XO. Dunning's only explanation was, "It is his style. Get used to it!" I might have gotten used to it had it not been for the fitness report (evaluation) I received from MacDonald in December 1982; less than six months after his taking command.

Just before Christmas 1982, I received a call from the Admin Officer to come to the captain's office. When I got to the captain's ante-room, I was told, "Sit down and read this!" To my surprise, it was a fitness report. The report was based upon four and a half months of serving PAO, under Captain MacDonald.

When I reviewed the grades, I saw it was a 5%, the worse in the command! When I had a chance to speak directly to the captain, his only comment was, "I like to give challenges."

Soon after, I began receiving calls from acquaintances on the Chief of Information's staff in Washington warning me that MacDonald was doing with me the same thing he had done to Ford. That is, he was expressing his displeasure and seeking my transfer. When I called the PAO detailer, Commander Arthur Norton, seeking guidance on how to handle the problem, his advice was "Try harder to please your CO." Matters only got worse for all the minority officers.

During subsequent staff meetings, the harassment and questions increased to the point, that on several occasions, meetings had to be paused because either LCDR Regan or LT Vaughn had been brought to tears by the captain's biting remarks.

The worst of those sessions took place in one particular meeting when the captain ordered LT Vaughn to leave immediately on a TAD trip. When she questioned if he meant in the morning? He replied, "No, I want you to leave right now."

Vaughn tried to explain to him that as a single parent with an adopted daughter, it would be near impossible to get a sitter on such notice. In the past when she had travelled, she could rely on being given at least a day to acquire a babysitter. No notice babysitters were hard to come by.

The captain refused to relent and angrily replied, "I want you gone!" He went on, 'No one told you to go get a child without a husband." As Vaughn sat there stunned and tearing up, he concluded, "I want you out of here. If you cannot travel when I want you to, what good are you to me?"

When Vaughn returned from that particular road trip, the captain assigned her to Navy Recruiting District Chicago, Glenview, IL, on no cost orders. Vaughn spent the remainder of her tour as the Area Minority Recruiting Officer in the NRD. Eventually, Vaughn resigned her commission and left the Navy.

In light of events involving Ford, Regan, and Vaughn, LT Roach and I decided to meet the captain's challenge of "What have you done?" by making it a point to remind him that he had an open invitation to attend all our monthly community meetings.

The meetings involved the Defense Advisory Committee On Women In the Services, Chicago Area Golden Thirteen, World War II Black Veterans of Great Lakes, Navy League, American Legion, and Veterans of Foreign Wars. Occasionally, we met with local scouting and drill teams, all in the name of maintaining a Navy Recruiting Area Five presence. Despite our open invitations, he rarely attended. But his sarcasm continued.

After one meeting with DACOWITS, which he did attend, he challenged LT Roach, asking, "What have those girls done to help you in recruiting?" It did not matter to him that several of the "girls" were Navy commanders and captains whom he saw and interacted with regularly during station leadership meetings, at other functions, or when he or his family visited the hospital.

When it came to the meetings of the World War II Black

Veterans of Great Lakes, the Golden Thirteen, and other meetings with Black Men or organizations, his remarks were just as offensive as those towards the DACOWITS; asking me after one meeting, "What have those old Black guys done to help you in your work?"

In an effort to preclude those kinds of questions, I doubled down on my invites for him to meet with the various groups. One particular local group that was more akin to our recruiting was the Angel Drill Team.

The Angel Drill Team had been founded in 1971 by a retired Navy Master Chief, Nathaniel Hamilton. Initially, the drill team was open to both boys and girls. However, by the time I arrived in Great Lakes, its forte was the involvement of girls ages 10 to 16 from North Chicago, Waukegan, Gurnee, Zion, Grayslake and Great Lakes. The group performed military style precision marching and rifle twirling.

Hamilton's sole purpose in creating the team was to attract young people to join the Navy. Over the years, Angel Drill Team was credited with putting many young people into the Navy.

On base at Great Lakes and throughout the surrounding area, Chief Hamilton and the Angel Drill Team were frequent guests and participated in many base and community functions. Despite McDonald knowing this, he never came to any of their competitions or recognized them for the work they did to assist local recruiting.

After one of our staff meetings, when he asked me once again, "What have those old Black men and that drill team done to help you in your work?" I replied, "Those old men and the drill team have done more to benefit NRD Chicago and Area Five than most any groups recently. My office has been very instrumental in keeping them involved." His only comment, "Then you should give them to the NRD to work!" I could only shake my head in disbelief.

Not long after that conversation, LCDR Reagan retired. About a month later, LT Roach's active-duty orders were terminated. In less than a year, Captain McDonald had manipulated the turnover of his entire minority officer staff.

My tour in Great Lakes was to have been three years. When MacDonald reported onboard, I was two years into my tour and due for orders. In anticipation and to preclude further damage to my career, I called the PAO Detailer to see if there was a possibility of leaving sooner. What I received was a tirade about attempting to detail from the field. I was told not only would I not get orders, but my tour was being extended.

To my surprise, he also added, that while the Golden Thirteen cruise had been a success, it had shown the Chief, Navy Office of Information, Rear Admiral Jack Garrow, that I was not a team player. And it had been successful despite me.

Norton concluded by letting me know that he, MacDonald, and the Chief of Information, Rear Admiral Garrow had engaged in detailed conversations as to what to do with me.

In October 1983, MacDonald assigned me no cost orders to Navy Recruiting District Glenview. My interim commanding officer was Captain J. D. Furnbach. The captain and I had discussed ways in which to use the Golden Thirteen and involve the Angel Drill Team in more local activities. While I was pleased to get away from MacDonald, and going to work for Furnbach, I was not happy with how my career was going.

I was reminded of my displeasure each morning when I drove my personal vehicle on base to the Area Five office in Great Lakes, picked up a recruiting vehicle, and drove approximately twenty-five miles down to Glenview. To arrive at Glenview on time at 0800, I had to leave my house by 0630 every morning. To turn the Navy vehicle in on time, I had to leave Glenview each day around 1600 to drop the car off before 1800.

Over the next six or so months, I had just three personal contacts with Captain MacDonald. One was when he ordered me to drop by his office to brief him on the person whom he learned was replacing me.

My replacement, Lieutenant Nettie Johnson, a black female, was new to recruiting. In all honesty, I had met her once, but I was not about to provide him "intelligence" upon which he could harm her. I told him that I knew little about her beyond where she went to school, her rank and her experience in Public Affairs. That did not satisfy him.

He then began to question me about her married life. To which, I told him I knew nothing about her personal life.

After several minutes of grilling on other aspects of Nettie's personal life, he abruptly concluded the meeting, saying,

"That is one of your problems, you have no loyalty to your commanding officer." I asked, "Do you have anything else for me?" When he did not answer, I went on, "If not, with your permission, I would like to leave." I got up and left.

Years later, when I related that conversation to Karen Roach, she told me of a similar conversation she had with MacDonald where he felt it was his duty to critique her on her marriage. I could only shake my head in disbelief. Right under his nose, his executive officer, John Dunning, who was separated but not divorced, was openly shacking with Petty Officer Thompson. Each morning, the two drove into the office in her car!

Soon after the Johnson conversation, I had my second in-person encounter with MacDonald. It was during that meeting I was informed I was being transferred to the staff of the Chief of Information.

As I was leaving, MacDonald decided he would say one more thing to me. As I stood to leave, he said, "I have honestly tried my best to make a better officer of you." He continued, "I have struggled with you and for the life of me cannot understand why you never responded." He went on, "I am baffled why I did not get any reaction out of you." Finally, he said, "I have seen better men succumb to a heart attack under the kind of pressure I have placed on you!"

Thoroughly angry, I stood and said, "Maybe the good lord did not intend for a man like you to break a man like me!" Without saying a word further, and with my stomach aching worse than I had ever experienced, I got up and left his office.

I went home and related the conversation to my wife. Like me, she had nothing to say in the face of such evil!

In February 1984, I received orders to the staff of CHINFO. The explanation was that I was being recalled to Washington to ascertain my suitability to be a naval officer. My third and final encounter with MacDonald came when I went by to receive my detaching 30% fitness report that covered the fourteen-month period from my last report in December 1982 to March 1984.

If there was a bright spot in that report, it was that I received a 1% concurrent fitness report for a portion of that time from NRD Chicago skipper, Captain J.D. Firnbach. The Firnbach report had been folded into the MacDonald document. When I saw the MacDonald evaluation, I was shocked, saddened, and depressed.

As I stood there trying to read the report, he interrupted me and said, "Your problem is you ran into someone who had previous public affairs experience. You see, I used to be a collateral duty PAO when I was an ensign" I thought to myself, "How fucking delusional. An ensign collateral duty PAO bears no resemblance to what I was doing as an echelon three PAO." MacDonald concluded, "Read it, sign it, and get out!" I signed the document, took my copy, and left.

As I left the office, I felt worse than the day he had berated me and sarcastically opined why I had not succumbed to a heart attack. I had never dreamed one could receive such a report. I later learned that McDonald had issued at least two other such reports to Lieutenants Vaughn and Roach upon their departures.

Chapter 5

DC

In Washington, I met with RADM Jack Garrow, Chief of Information, and was told that my being in Washington was an opportunity for me to prove my credentials as a public affairs officer. Further, the admiral reassured me that what happened in Great Lakes would have no bearing on my activities in DC and my salvaging what might be left of my career. I honestly believed him.

My initial assignments while on the staff of the Chief of Information were to represent the Navy on two boards examining minority recruiting endeavors and coordinating the CHINFO briefing for the Portuguese equivalent of the Chief of Naval Operations.

The Wall Street firm of Booze-Allen was responsible for the minority recruiting endeavor. Specifically, they were examining issues surrounding the quality of NROTC programs at historically black colleges. Upon completion of both, which kept me away from the office for nearly a year, I received letters of commendation for my work on both assignments.

The letters were incorporated into a 10% fitness report from RADM Garrow: the lowest in the command. During the personal debrief of his 10% fitness report, the admiral let me know, "I called the grades as I saw them."

As I was leaving the admiral's office, there was much laughter, glad handing, and back slapping among my peers who had received "better" FITREPs. That day, I foolishly left the office early without saying a word to a soul. The reality of my situation was sinking in. I needed the time to myself. The next morning, no one bothered to inquire about my where-abouts. Soon after, my record containing the detrimental MacDonald and Garrow fitness reports went before my first Lieutenant Commander selection board. I was passed over for promotion.

After receiving official notification of my non-selection for promotion, I began inquiring of Navy Legal, Navy Military Personnel Command (NMPC) and the National Naval Officers Association about the process of appealing a pass-over for promotion. I was absolutely appalled by the lack of information and guidance from all three. The best advice I received came from Navy Legal, which was, "you really need a civilian attorney if you expect success." That advice proved worthless when I asked, "*Can you recommend someone?*" Their response? "*We don't provide lists or recommendations of attorneys. You will have to do your own research.*" NMPC provided similar advice. NNOA never returned my call. I began reaching out to civilian attorneys.

My quest to find a civilian attorney was as depressing as dealing with military administrative personnel. Frequently, civilian attorneys made remarks akin to, "*The Navy is changing. Based upon what I have seen, they need (black) people like you to show they are making progress in race relations.*" One attorney offered proof by referring to the "*recent at sea reunion of the first Black naval officers!*" I could not help but recognize the irony in that remark.

There I was, the Black officer who originated the idea of the 1982 Golden Thirteen reunion at sea, being told that the reunion was proof that the Navy was changing.

I felt like a damned fool. As the saying goes, "I not only drank the Kool-Aid. I drained the pitcher!" Despite such statements and my personal feelings, I pressed on.

After three months of looking, I finally located a law firm willing to take my case. The firm, King and Eberhardt, was in Virginia near the Pentagon. The principle was an attorney by the name of Guy Ferrante. Based upon literature and word of mouth, the firm had been successful in dealing with military appeals, which included boards for promotion.

In our initial meeting, Ferrante made it clear that the fight would be difficult but winnable. He cautioned me that we should allow the Navy the opportunity to deal internally with the matter before going outside of the service. Reluctantly, I agreed.

Following the lead of my attorney, I filed a request with the Board for Correction of Naval Records for removal of the Passovers due to the MacDonald and Garrow fitness reports because they did not reflect my actual performance of duty. That petition was dismissed for lack of documentation.

In the meantime, at CHINFO, I was assigned to be the Deputy Assistant to the Director of Community Relations, Office of the Navy Chief of Information. My immediate supervisor, the Director of Community Relations, was Commander Frederic Leeder, who quickly assigned me to full time duties as the CHINFO Public Affairs Officer for the 75th Anniversary of Naval Aviation. Although I was technically still assigned to the staff of the Chief of Information, Community Relations at the Pentagon, my duty station was the Washington Navy Yard. I was pleased to get away from the Pentagon and what I saw as the toxic atmosphere of the CHINFO office.

My immediate supervisor on the committee was Captain Rosario "Zip" Rausa, a naval aviator who flew 150 combat missions in Vietnam.

The work of the committee included coordinating local activities involving the 75th Anniversary with committee headquarters located in Pensacola, FL. The highlight of the DC Committee's activities included a painting featuring the Vice President George Bush as he was being rescued after being downed during WWII and the NC-4 Transatlantic reenact flight.

During the Washington, DC leg of the trip, celebrations were conducted at NAS Andrews. It was my responsibility to consult with other military units, reporting suggestions and results back to the committee and CHINFO leadership, Commander Leeder.

The height of the yearlong assignment was the day pilot and Texas millionaire, Wilson Connie Edwards, reenacted the

Navy transatlantic flight of the Curtiss NC-4, which took place in 1919, eight years before Charles Lindbergh made his famous crossing.

Edwards, with the blessing of the Navy, reenacted the flight in his personal restored plane, Catalina PBY. He followed the same route as the 1919 flight, beginning in Pensacola, FL on to Washington, DC, Rockaway, New York, and on to Nova Scotia, Newfoundland, the Azores, and finally ending the flight in Plymouth, England. My involvement ended when the plane departed for New York.

However, my yearlong involvement in the project and its subsequent success, prompted the project supervisor, Captain Rausa, to forward up the chain a 1% concurrent fitness report. The report was drafted, passed to my CHINFO supervisor for review and concurrence, and sent to the Deputy Chief of Naval Operations for Air Warfare, Vice Admiral Edward Martin, for approval and signing.

When I learned that Commander Leeder had accepted it and passed it along to Admiral Garrow, my spirits soared because I realized that such a FITREP could help salvage my career. However, what happened next made it clear that my days in the Navy were definitely over.

Just after the drafting of the Vice Admiral Martin FITREP, I received a call from the senior reserve PAO on the 75th Anniversary Committee, Captain Eugene Cagle. In the call, he related a conversation he had had with then Commander in Chief US Atlantic Fleet(CINCLANT), PAO Arthur Norton. Norton had previously been the PAO detailer and involved in the events concerning Great Lakes, Captain

MacDonald, and me.

The call had been precipitated because Cagle and I were having considerable difficulties getting support for the 75th project from various public affairs elements, among them CINCLANT.

In a 9 May 1988 letter from Eugene Cagle, Captain, USNR-Ret. PAO, Deputy Chief of Naval Operations (Air Warfare (OP-05D) 75th Anniversary of Naval Aviation, May 1985 to September 1986), Cagle recounted a bitter encounter with the former Detailer, Office of the Chief of Information, Commander Art Norton. He wrote, "In October/November 1985, the staff experienced some difficulty in obtaining support from various Navy public affairs field elements. One problem involved the staff of the Commander-In-Chief US Atlantic Fleet (CINCLANTFLT)." "…LT Collins took the matter up with his 75th Anniversary superiors who contacted CINCLANTFLT. The CINCLANTFLT contact, CDR Arthur Norton, called me in an effort to resolve the problem. During the course of the conversation, the Commander asked if there was a CHINFO staff member coordinating our activities. I answered, yes, and stated that LT Collins was that person." The Cagle letter goes on, "At the mention of LT Collins' name, CDR Norton proceeded to tell me, unsolicited, that he now understood why we had had problems. He stated that LT Collins was a known incompetent and was "not long for the Navy. He concluded by telling me that the Lieutenant was probably the cause of our problems and that we'd be better off without him."

Cagle continued, "The most disturbing aspect of the Commander's remarks was the fact that we did not know each other. That he would render such a vicious unsolicited attack on a fellow naval officer was appalling. It was quite obvious to me that he did not have the Lieutenant's best interests at heart."

Cagle related the contents of the conversation to me, Commander Leeder, and to RADM Jack Garrow, Chief of Information, and concluded this part of his letter by stating "Norton apologized to me. His apology, however, was forced; the tenor of the conversation was basically angry."

Cagle concluded his letter with, "After learning of the Lieutenant's difficulties, it became apparent to me that the situation involving CDR Norton was probably more serious than I first thought. If he were willing to say such adverse things to me, a stranger, what had he said to the Chief of Information, whom he knew quite well and briefed frequently...I believe It is indicative of a larger problem which impacted an officer's career."

I was more angry than surprised at the comments attributed to Norton because he had made it clear to me what his desires were for me before my leaving Great Lakes.

Soon after learning of that conversation, Garrow refused to accept the DCNO Air Warfare proposed 1% concurrent FITREP. He issued me a 5% FITREP incorporating the Martin proposed report. It was the worst in the command.

Shortly afterward, my record went before the Board for Selection. As Norton had predicted, I was passed over for promotion.

Chapter 6

The Aftermath

In May 1986, Admiral Garrow retired. On his way out, he awarded me a 1% FITREP, again the worst in the command. Simultaneously, I received notification of my pending discharge from active duty due to two failures to select for promotion.

In November 1986, I was discharged from the active Navy after fourteen years and eight months of active service. I had requested reserve augmentation, which was granted.

In February 1987, I was finally awarded the Navy Commendation Medal for my work on the 75th Anniversary of Naval Aviation. According to the accompanying citation, the period covered was October 1985 to November 1986; the same period of the proposed 1% fitness report forwarded to Rear Admiral Garrow by Vice Admiral Martin. The award was also accompanied by a letter from Garrow's immediate relief, Rear Admiral Jimmy Finklestein.

In May 1987, I was passed over for promotion in the reserves. At the time, I was on a temporary active-duty contract with

CHINFO. I had hoped that my continued active duty would help my chances for promotion in the reserves. I was wrong.

In September 1987, I submitted my second petition to the Board for Correction of Naval Records. I requested reinstatement to active duty, removal of the two fitness reports (5% and 30%) issued by MacDonald, removal of my pass overs for promotion, and removal of the 10% report from Garrow.

The basis for the request was collusion of commanding officers (MacDonald and Garrow) as evidenced by Commander Norton's actions and the discrimination and bigotry of MacDonald.

The request included supporting statements from the minority officers who had experienced the wrath of MacDonald. It graphically detailed his discrimination and concluded with the fact that in less than a year of his arrival, MacDonald had purged his staff of the four minority/ women officers who were in place when he arrived.

Detailed supporting documents also showed how MacDonald ignored obvious other infractions, which included accusations of fraternization and overlooking PT standards for obese members of the staff.

Previously, I pointed out that the entire time I was assigned to NRD Glenview, the executive officer, Commander Dunning and the senior enlisted person, Petty Officer First Class Sherri Thompson, openly lived together off base in North Chicago. Also, it was less than a secret throughout the command that Petty Officer Thompson's number was the only phone number used to contact the executive officer during off-duty hours.

The petition also detailed how, in ridding himself of his minority officers, MacDonald had frequently used less than favorable fitness reports as the mechanism to destroy or damage careers.

When the petition went forward to the Board, I questioned my attorney's not making a reference to specific discrimination statutes in the accusations. Ferrante's response was, "If the Navy has the will to correct acts of discrimination, I believe the overwhelming evidence of discrimination and bigotry should be enough." I accepted his explanation.

In May 1988, I was passed over for a second time in the reserves and notified of my pending discharge from the reserves.

In September 1988, as I was finishing a second and final temporary active duty on the staff of the Chief of Information, and facing release from the reserves, I received a letter from then CHINFO, RADM Finklestein. In it, he referred to my work on the 75th Anniversary of Naval Aviation and my tenure as his Assistant Director for Community Relations.

The letter said, "Lieutenant Collins' performance of duty was excellent." The letter went on, "Lieutenant Collins is a fine public affairs officer. When he left active duty, the Navy lost an excellent officer. I would be pleased to have him serve on my staff again."

Dumbfounded, I passed the information to my attorney.

In December 1988, I was notified through my attorney that the Board for Corrections had returned my petition to NMPC-22 with the recommendation that the two FITREPs from MacDonald for the period 27 August 1982 through 31 Dec 1982 and 1 January 1983 to February 1984, be removed. The explanation was that the board did not believe MacDonald had fairly assessed my performance.

Following is a summation of the letter, dated 23 December 1988, recommending partial reconsideration. In the letter, the Board removed a fitness report, awarded just before my first board for promotion to Lieutenant Commander. As a result of the removal, a hole was left in my record. The existence of the hole connotes that there was something amiss. Holes in records are not normal. That same letter refers to another fitness report written by the same individual, which the board did not remove. However, the discussion of that report verifies that there was controversy surrounding all the evaluations written by that one individual. Again, the fact that there was a statement discussing the necessity not to remove that evaluation also belies the reviewer's statements and gives credence to the existence of my "self-reported" stressors.

In ordering the removal of that one evaluation, the letter stated, "*the board still concurs with the contents of NMPC-32 opinion...in finding the existence of an injustice warranting the removal of the fitness report for 1 January 1983 to February 29, 1984.*" The Board added, "*The Board again finds that this reporting senior exhibited "overkill" in downgrading the petitioner in the report ending 29 February 1984.*"

NMPC-32 made it clear it was that specific reporting senior (MacDonald) who precipitated an ongoing stressful environment that continued after my transfer to Washington and throughout the last two years of my active-duty career. The ripple effect of his actions tainted all my fitness reports and boards going forward.

The board's decision was made primarily based upon a detailed letter of support written by Commander Thomas Wyld, one of the senior Navy Recruiting Command PAOs, who had supported my idea for the Golden Thirteen Cruise and had been intimately involved in its coming about.

Wyld was familiar with the frequent unsolicited calls from MacDonald in his efforts to purge both Lieutenant Roach and me from his staff.

In its decision, issued 14 February 1989, the Board did not support removal of the Garrow fitness report, nor the removal of my two failures to promote active-duty boards. It also let stand the 5% report from MacDonald. The explanation: "*A 5% fitness report, in and of itself, is not an adverse report.*"

In the same request, the Board had asked NMPC-61 (EO) to comment on the accusations of discrimination made by my petition. It also gave MacDonald an opportunity to respond to the request for removal of his fitness reports.

In his response, MacDonald further disparaged me and insinuated that Captain Firnbach, CO NRD Chicago, the individual who had provided me a concurrent 1% report, had agreed with him in assessing me. He also went as far as to name individuals to whom he had spoken.

One of them happened to be LCDR Charles (Chuck) Connor, the individual who had been assigned to the Navy Chicago Office of Information for a number of years and bragged about his relationship with one of the Golden Thirteen, Justice Sylvester White. Chuck was one of those who attacked the Golden Thirteen reunion idea as not worthy of pursuing and had expressed a similar thought to RADM Jack Garrow. The other person MacDonald cited in his correspondence who could "vouch" for his struggles with me was a reserve captain, Sam Sax.

Sax and I rarely had contact with each other. He was most noteworthy to me and my staff because, at the time of his promotion to captain, he had gone to the Great Lakes Navy Exchange, ordered a new uniform, picked it up and walked off without paying for it.

It was my office that assisted the Exchange in identifying him and played a part in his not being charged with shoplifting.

The final person cited by MacDonald as being able to vouch for his struggles with me was, Captain Firnbach, the skipper of Naval Recruiting District Chicago. As I have noted, Captain Firnbach had frequent involvement in the local Golden Thirteen and World War II Black Veterans of Great Lakes meetings arranged by my office. Often, it was Firnbach who represented the Area Commander at those meetings because MacDonald did not have time nor interest.

In March 1989, with no response from NMPC-61, I reached out to Captain Gordon Peterson, an acquaintance from Recruiting Command. He in-turn reached out to NMPC – EO.

In the interim, I wrote to NMPC-22 seeking an explanation as to why EO had not responded to the accusations of discrimination. I received no response.

I decided to take the matter higher. I wrote to Admiral Boorda based upon my having read the 1988 CNO Study of EO in the Navy, which found:

- *Minority fitness report grades were lower resulting in lower selection rates for minority promotions.*

- *Although no reason for lower grades could be discerned, it concluded the rates were due to bias.*

- *Promotion/screening boards were not provided sufficient information concerning Navy EO goals for higher minority representation at senior grades.*

Regarding NMPC-61, the 1988 CNO study stated the Equal Opportunity Division did not perform many of its assigned tasks, among them:

- *It did not monitor minority officer assignments, career progression or provide career counseling.*

- *It did not evaluate the effectiveness of the Navy Affirmative Action Plan.*

- *It did not coordinate recommendations for revision of the Affirmative Action Plan.*

- It did not review or evaluate assessment reports for progress in Equal Opportunity.

Soon after writing to Admiral Boorda, I made an unannounced call to the EO Office. At the time, the Director was Captain Pete Tzomes. I was not expecting Tzomes, because when I had originally submitted my request, the acting director was Commander David Brewer. I had met him while he was going through hot-plant training at Great Lakes.

When I filed my petition with a copy to EO, Brewer had assured me that the matter would be looked into promptly. Apparently, it never happened.

When Captain Tzomes and I met, he told me he had received a copy of my concerns expressed to Captain Gordon. Further, he emphatically stated that his office had not received any request from NMPC-22. He also let me know that he knew Captain MacDonald because they were both members of the submarine community.

Not long after my visit to NMPC-61, I received a letter dated 10 April 1989 from Captain Tzomes, in which he restated what we discussed and concluded: "*You have exercised your right to present your case to the BCNR ...the board responded with their recommendations to the Assistant Secretary of the Navy who in turn approved those recommendations.*" There was no reference to his having stated to me that he had known MacDonald for some time.

In July 1989, I received correspondence from VADM Boorda in which he explained "why" NMPC-61 had not responded to the tasking originally given by NMPC-22 in February that year.

The Boorda letter stated, "*I have looked into the matters you addressed and have not found any improprieties affecting the processing and outcome of your case nor any clear indications of discrimination.*"

The letter went on, "*Though true that the Equal Opportunity Division, Naval Military Personnel Command (NMPC-61), did not investigate nor comment on matters "administratively" referred to them by the Military Personnel Evaluations Division, Naval Military Personnel Command (NMPC-32), such an omission had no impact on the decision of the Board for Correction of Naval Records (BCNR). The BCNR assigned a disinterested Equal Employment Opportunity Specialist to the panel which conducted a thorough review of your petition and determined that an advisory opinion from NMPC-61 was not necessary.*"

The letter continued, "*In spite of the above action, I requested NMPC-61 to examine your case file and, to the extent possible, determine whether or not discrimination existed. Based upon this review, your current claim of discrimination could not be established.*"

The Admiral closed letting me know that he was aware of my contact with Captain Tzomes and suggested I bring to him or Tzomes any more information I might have.

In January 1990, I received a final letter from VADM Boorda. In it, he stated that the review he had ordered after my contact with his office had resulted in another review. This time, the review involved the entire fitness report writing history of MacDonald, from 1982-1985, and included twenty-six officers: both black and white, male, and female.

The letter said, "*What emerged was an image of Captain MacDonald as a tough, but fair commander who told it like it was: Interested in details; expected to be kept informed; fair, honest, moral; and one who expected the complete support of his staff. There were no indications of discrimination against you or other officers on the basis of race or other discernible factors."*

Sadly, when I reached out to the other minority officers who received career damaging fitness reports from MacDonald at the same time as I did, only one had been contacted; Lieutenant Ford, the aviator. If you recall, he had been the first officer transferred early in the tenure of Captain MacDonald. His transfer, which came nearly a year before his tour was scheduled to end, was seen by others and me as a rescue by his detailer.

Once again, I reached out to VADM Boorda, but never heard from him. I was disappointed because I wanted to believe in VADM Boorda.

Two of the strongest support letters demonstrating potential collusion between Captain MacDonald and the Chief of Information were provided by Captains Rosario "Zip" Rausa and Frederick Leader.

In a letter dated 18 October 1989 and provided to the board and VADM Boorda, Captain Rosario M. Rausa, USNR (Ret), formerly of the Staff DCNO Air Warfare, January 1985 to December 1985, recounted a conversation with the Chief of Information, Admiral Jack Garrow, informing him that his office intended to forward a favorable evaluation which would have helped ensure that I received credit for my exemplary performance while working with him and the Air Warfare staff.

Rausa recalled *"after forwarding to Admiral Jack Garrow a concurrent 1% evaluation which was to have been signed by the Chief of Naval Operations, Air Warfare, Admiral James D. Watkins, USN, "I was advised by the Chief of Information that the fitness report would not be accepted." Rausa went on, "I was stunned as I had never experienced a situation whereby praise, in the form of a fitness report, would not (be) permitted."*

In the second letter, written during the same period, similar actions on the part of the Chief of Information were reported in correspondence provided to both BCNR and ADM Boorda.

The second letter, dated 17 November 1989, was written by Captain Frederic Leeder, USN SACLANT PAO – Former Director Chief of Information, Community Relations – 1986. His letter stated, *"Lieutenant Collins was assigned to me to fill the requirement for a full-time public affairs specialist to represent me and CHINFO on the staff of the 75th Anniversary of Naval Aviation…LT Collins did a superb job in every aspect. The job required working for two bosses, essentially, and I encouraged the 75th Anniversary staff to write a concurrent fitness report on LT Collins which I found out they were planning to do anyway because they were extremely pleased with his performance."* Leader continued, *"With almost 16 years in Navy Public Affairs at the time, I felt he was doing 4.0/early promotion work as compared with other specialists of his grade. Accordingly, I submitted a draft fitness report up the chain of command for CHINFO (RADM Garrow's) signature with the recommendation that LT Collins be given top marks. As I recall, his fitrep for that period (late spring) was not as high as I had recommended, and I was quite displeased and perplexed that he had been marked down from what I had submitted. In fact, I also recall that I had been asked (before the command's fitreps for that grade were signed and distributed) if I REALLY wanted to mark LT Collins as I had recommended, in view of his previous record performance. My response was that "I called it as I saw it," (I) didn't care what he may or may not have done in previous duties and would not care to change my recommendation."*

Soon after those series of letters and my last correspondence with Boorda, I received a call from Captain Tzomes. The purpose of his call was, as he put it, *"To give me some Dutch uncle advice."* He went on, *"In future, you should spend more time doing your job rather than bitching and moaning about how white people are fucking you over."* I hung up, not wanting to engage in a call not to my benefit.

Reluctantly, I began turning my interests to other areas. The decision was necessary because not only was I out of work, but I had also spent my entire severance pay on legal fees.

In my last conversation with my attorney, Guy Ferrante, he expressed disappointment too at the outcome of events. As he put it, *"We proved that the decision to remove the MacDonald 30% report was a right one."* He went on, *"Why they did not remove his 5% is beyond me. Removal of both would have necessitated the invalidation of your boards."* He concluded, *"It would have at least put you in the zone for retirement from the reserves if not active duty."*

Ferrante went on, *"Regarding our accusations of discrimination, the fact that the captain had precipitated the removal or transfer of five minority and women officers should have been proof of his bigotry. For the Navy to have wanted more from you, the victim, is unbelievable."*

He continued, "*With the work you did for the Golden Thirteen, and for them to have rendered such a bad decision at a time when they claimed they want more minority officers, is further proof of their insincerity and unwillingness to change.*"

Finally, he opined, "*I must conclude, the Navy decided it would have been too costly to attempt to salvage your career. They removed the worst of the fitness reports, and let stand your pass-overs for promotion and discharge. They did the least they could without disrupting the system.*"

Chapter 7

Today and Tomorrow

Throughout my tour as a naval officer, the thing I most resented was hearing people refer to blacks and other minorities as affirmative action hires. When I returned to active duty, it was because I found something I thought the navy wanted and could use: *an officer with a media public relations background.* Seeing Admiral Zumwalt's encouraging messages and hearing first hand of the changes he had made made my return to active duty an easy decision.

To this day, I am extremely proud of my personal struggle to become a naval officer despite not having gone through a source program. I struggled and passed all the classes needed to become an officer. No one gave me anything.

When I assumed the role of Public Affairs Officer, Navy Recruiting Area Five, I was the only minority in such a prestigious national position. According to the publicity and verbiage of the Navy at that time, I should have been seen as an asset. Yet internal to the Navy, I was not. Instead, I was seen as a black man engaged in black things.

For example, once, as part of my recruiting duties, I was tasked to go to New York to preview a proposed minority recruiting ad. When asked my opinion of the ad, I stated that I found the ad unrealistic because of its use of what the creators identified as "black slang."

During the ensuing heated conversation, I was accused of being disrespectful, ordered to apologize, and threatened with being sent back to my Region. In the interim, my boss, Captain DiLorenzo, was called. After a conversation with her, I apologized.

As that was taking place, one officer, Lieutenant Commander Mike Labbe, stepped forward and defended my conduct. He stated, "Jerry was asked his opinion of the ad. He provided it in a very respectful manner." Labbe went on, "He gave an honest opinion which the contractor disagreed with." As a result, others on the review committee came to my defense. Before I apologized, I asked how I was disrespectful. No one could give me an explanation beyond challenging my knowledge of "black slang." The matter did not end there.

I learned that later, Labbe was dressed down for his supporting "that black officer's" disrespectful disruption. Labbe and I would later conclude that the point of my critique was missed because of "who" raised it. Just after my return to Recruiting Area Five following the New York incident, I had another incident that reminded me of the Ad Agency event.

The idea of a Golden Thirteen at sea Reunion was presented to the Navy Office of Information, Chicago, deputy, LCDR Connor. He dismissed it as little more than a stunt to garner attention for me. He added, "I have known and had relationships for some time with Johnson Publishing Company and Golden Thirteen members, Justice Sylvester White and Jesse Arbor. If the idea had been worthwhile or worthy of pursuing, I am sure they, like me, would have recognized it long before you came along." I pressed on with the idea.

When I arrived in Norfolk for the actual reunion, I had nearly forgotten about the NAVINFO Chicago reaction.

At CINCLANT Public Affairs, Commander Kendal Pease, the PAO dismissed the idea too as little more than a "Nice Negro Story." His comments made it clear, the real issue was a lack of interest in anything historical that might promote black contributions to Navy history.

Pease's added comment that only the "Negro media" would be interested in the story fueled my determination to "paper tidewater" with press releases about the upcoming cruise and led me to the UPI desk hidden away in the stairwell of the Virginian Pilot-Ledger Star building.

Hidden in my records to the BCNR is a letter dated 16 September 1988 from Captain MacDonald. Like the actions of both Connor and Pease, it is noteworthy because it attacks my competence as a minority, an officer, and indeed a public affairs officer. And, it is representative of the contempt and racism that too many minorities have had to contend with as we attempted to make progress in our Navy careers.

Contained in the MacDonald letter is the statement: "*He (Lieutenant Collins) impressed me as being cleverly manipula-*

*tive of the system. Specifically, when under the pressure of the mission, he was **dilatory**."*

From the times of slavery, blacks have had to contend with code words. I contend "dilatory" is one of those words. A review of synonyms for dilatory reveals a multiplicity of buzz words often used to defame blacks and other minorities. Among those synonyms are words like laggard, lazy, neglectful, and slacker. I believe the Board recognized Mac-Donald's actions in the use of that word.

In its opinion regarding the recommendation for the removal of MacDonald's fitness reports, "the board concurred with the contents of NMPC-32 opinion *"in finding the existence of an injustice warranting the removal of the fitness report for 1 January 1983 to February 29 1984, because the reporting senior exhibited overkill in downgrading the petitioner (LT Collins) in the report ending 29 February 1984.* It is not a stretch to further conclude that MacDonald's use of the word dilatory is just another racist attempt to further besmirch my reputation as both an officer and a public affairs specialist.

Earlier, I wrote that I still have an affinity for Dennis Nelson and what he attempted to do. Despite the reaction by some to the 1982 Golden Thirteen Reunion Cruise at its inception and conclusion, and because of the successful reunion onboard USS KIDD, I take pride in knowing that at least once, I took part and played a lead role in helping to publicize the accomplishments of one group of naval pioneers.

Despite what happened to my career because of animus and bigotry, I am extremely proud of my near seventeen and a half years of active duty and reserve service. If in the beginning, someone had told me how things would turn out, I would have still undertaken the challenge of helping to bring the Golden Thirteen Story out of the shadows.

I take a great deal of satisfaction from the pictures I have. And there is one thing in particular that gives me great satisfaction and reassures me each time I read it.

In April, just after the conclusion of the cruise, I received a personal letter written by Mr. John Reagan. In the letter, dated April 27 1982, Mr. Reagan wrote, "*I am still 10 kilometers high from that terrific "Golden Thirteen" reunion at sea. It is near impossible to express how much I appreciated the terrific job you did with and for us and indeed for the Navy and recruiting service.*"

The letter concludes, "*I took the liberty of penning a note of gratitude to CO of District Five.... Jerry, thanks again. Keep up the good work! Cordially, JR.*"

I never saw nor received a copy of the letter Mr. Reagan wrote to "*CO District Five.*"

As I began writing my story, I also came across another letter written by Commander Thomas Wyld, former Special Assistant for Public Affairs to both RADM F. H. Miller and later RADM J. D. Williams, the Commander Navy Recruiting Command. The letter, dated 5 September 1986, answered many questions and specifically the question of "*Which Negro Press would cover the reunion at sea?*"

In that letter, submitted to the Board of Correction of Naval Records, Wyld stated, "*When I met Lieutenant Collins, he was trying to interest senior leadership in supporting an idea of his: a reunion of the Navy's first Black Officers. Such an event, he believed, would attract media attention and boost awareness in the one recruitment market that was needed the most: the Black Officer Market. Lieutenant Collins convinced recruiting leadership to support his idea and nurtured the project every step of the way, from conception to media escort duties at sea. The result was the historic reunion...an...event, covered by every major national media—including the New York Times, CBS, and ABC and most importantly by virtually every Black medium in the United States. Lieutenant Collins was personally commended by the Chief of Naval Operations,...hailed by the Assistant Secretary of Defense for Equal Opportunity... because the story made a compelling statement of minority opportunities in the Armed Forces."*

The Wyld letter went on, "*The event not only built awareness, but also resulted in accessions. ROTC units at predominantly black colleges and universities were swamped with telephone call inquiries, and as were black newspapers that featured the story.*"

He also spoke of trainings I developed that resulted in other articles from my staff at Area Five that appeared in *Navy Recruiter*, the national recruiting magazine.

At this juncture in his letter, Wyld addressed the issues I encountered that directly impacted my career prior to leaving Great Lakes for Washington, DC and the Chief of Information staff. He stated, "*It is unfortunate...that Lieutenant Collins faced opposition in executing Command goals for improvements in public affairs activity and training.*" The letter goes on, "*Judging by the type and extent of tasks assigned that I would consider extraneous, I would say that his accomplishments in public affairs are truly remarkable."* Then Wyld elaborated on those extraneous things; *"items including elaborate shadow boxes, with crests and emblems, coffee cups, sweaters with insignia and the like... All required design work beyond the reasonable province of Navy public affairs work and all items were for the internal audience...not for the market in which recruiters must work. The items were of "questionable benefit to recruiter motivation and of no applicability to public affairs work."*

He went on, *"I included these specifics not to draw attention to possible irregularities, but simply to advise the Board that Lieutenant Collins was required to accomplish the extraordinary and the inappropriate while essentials---authorized public affairs initiatives of the Navy Recruiting Command among them—enjoyed no command priority or reinforcement."*

Wyld concluded his rather lengthy letter by stating, *"If I had to rank all twelve Public Affairs Officers who served at the Area staffs from 1981 to 1984, LT Collins would have been ranked number one of twelve, recommended for accelerated promotion...with all others ranked in lesser columns. I would be most pleased to serve with him again."*

In naval historian Paul Stillwell's 1986 book *The Golden Thirteen: Recollections of the First Black Naval Officers,* he describes Dennis Nelson *"as a man who would personally get involved when he believed that African Americans were underrepresented. As a result of his assertive and abrasive personality and equal rights advocacy, Nelson's superiors viewed him as a nuisance."*

In that statement, Stillwell makes it plain that Lieutenant Commander Dennis Nelson's relentless advocacy for integration and equality caused him to sacrifice advancement in his own naval career. In 1981, when I came up with the idea of an "at sea" reunion of the Golden Thirteen, there was little to nothing in print recognizing the accomplishments of those naval pioneers. Upon completion of the cruise, all of that changed. By the time Stillwell completed his book in 1986, numerous articles and other works about them had appeared in print.

Over the years since the reunion, my reunion cruise collaborator, Max Allen, and I have asked ourselves numerous times, "*was it coincidence that those articles, stories and books were written?*" Or was it just the right time for the telling of a "*Nice Negro Story: an American story?*

In retrospect, I have come to identify with Paul Stillwell's description of Lieutenant Commander Dennis Nelson and his personal sacrifice for the benefit of the Navy and others.

---GAC---

Photos

1978 California Recruiting Meeting the Men
First officially dubbed "The Golden Thirteen"
(NH 1234 courtesy Naval History & Heritage Com)

G-13 w/CNO Adm James Watkins
and CHINFO RADM Bruce Newell
(From Author's Collection)

G-13 Receiving Commemorative Poster
from SECNAV Hon. John Lehman
(From Author's Collection)

Author's Photo of Poster received from
SECNAV at 1982 Pentagon Luncheon
(Autographed at DC NNOA Reception)

USS KIDD DDG-993
Underway 1983 - Virginia Capes
(NH 1234 courtesy Naval History & Heritage Com)

Author being congratulated by SecNav John Lehman
"On A Job Well Done!"
(From Author's Photo Collection)

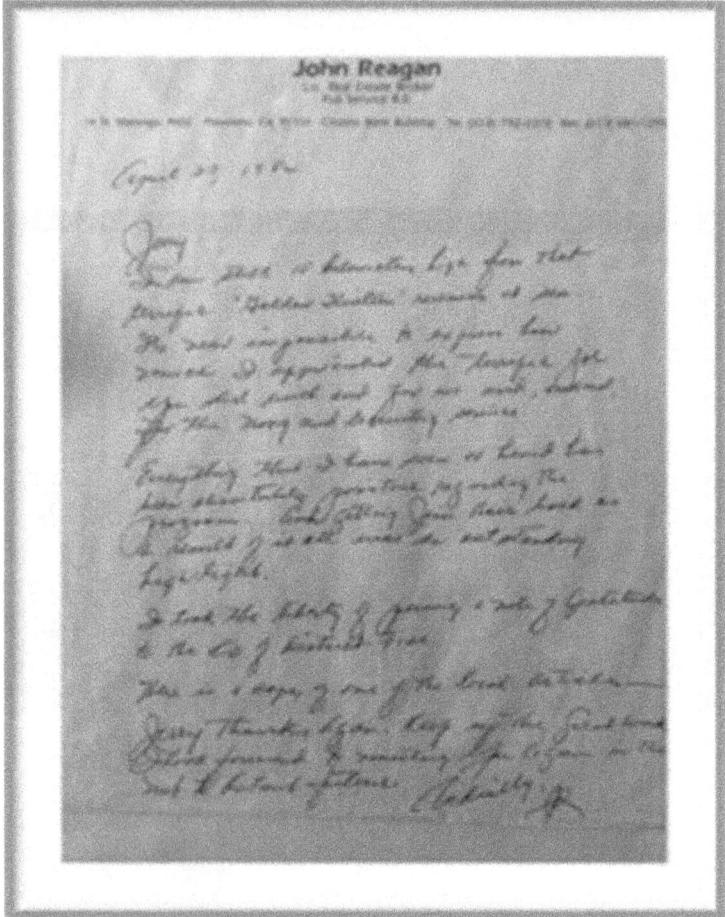

G13 Member John Reagan
"Thank You Letter" to Author
(From Author's Photo Collection)

"In The Shadow Of The Golden Thirteen-A Nice Negro Story"
In memory of the late
CDR Steve Pyles, USN-Ret. without whom there would have
been no Tidewater or DC NNOA receptions!

COMPANY	DATE OF COVERAGE	TYPE OF MEDIA
CBS Morning News	4/12/82 & 4/13/82	National Network News
Umoja Sasa	4/13/82	National Black Engineering Magazine
National Scene	4/13/82	Sunday Newspaper Supplement
Virginian Pilot	4/7/82 & 4/13/82	Newspaper (Norfolk)
Ledger Star	4/13/82 & 4/14/82	Newspaper (Norfolk)
Associated Press	4/8/82 & 4/13/82 4/14/82	Wire Service
New York Times	4/12/82 & 4/13/82	Newspaper
United Press Int.	4/13/82	Wire Service
WVEC TV 13	4/13/82 & 4/15/82	Television Station (ABC Affiliate and Cable News Network reciprocal)
WAVY TV 10	4/15/82	Television Station (NBC Affiliate)
Cox Broadcasting	4/13/82	Network Television/Radio
Sheridan Best	4/14/82	Radio Network (Remote from Ship)
Tennessee Radio Network	4/14/82	Radio Network (Remote from Ship)
WNIS Radio	4/14/82	Radio Station (Remote from Ship)Norfolk
WRAP Radio	4/14/82	Radio Station (Remote from Ship. National Black Network affiliate) Norfolk
WJPC Radio	4/14/82	Radio Station (Remote from Ship) Chicago
WWJ Radio	4/14/82	Radio Station (Remote from Ship) Detroit
WHIO Radio	4/14/82	Radio Station (Remote from Ship) Dayton
WDAO Radio	4/14/82	Radio Station (Remote from Ship) Dayton
WVOL Radio	4/14/82	Radio Station (Remote from Ship) Nashville
WIBC Radio	4/14/82	Radio Station (Remote from Ship) Indianapolis
WISE Radio	4/14/82	Radio Station (Remote from Ship) Indianapolis
WTLC Radio	4/14/82	Radio Station (Remote from Ship) Indianapolis

Partial List of "Negro Press" Covering
1982 G-13 USS KIDD at Sea Reunion

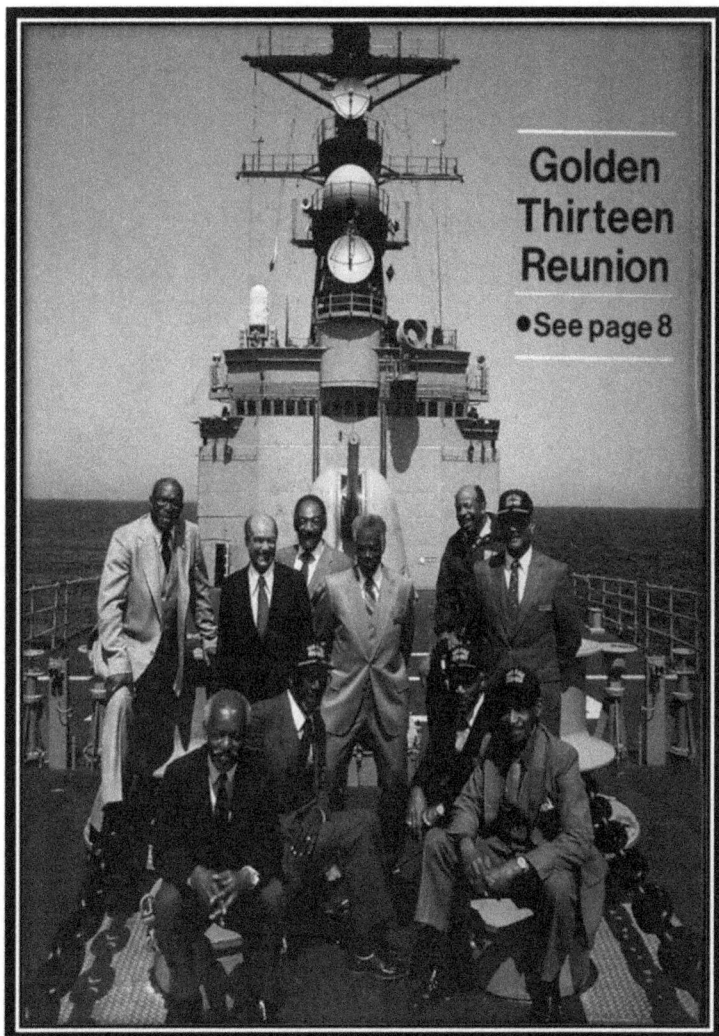

Back Cover "All Hands" Magazine – August 1982
(NH 1234 courtesy of the Naval History & Heritage Com)